AF257902

Man Of A Thousand Fails

Film Noir Of Elisha Cook Jr.

Opening Credits

The film is *Man of a Thousand Faces* 1957

Man Of A Thousand Fails

Film Noir Of Elisha Cook Jr.

First edition published in Australia, March 2026

by

Bent Banana Books
24 Lorraine Court
Lawnton, Australia, 4501.

Email bentbananabooks@gmail.com

Cover and layout designer: Bernardos!

ISBN: 978-1-7638100-5-1 Paperback

A CiP catalogue record for this book is available from the Australian National Library.

About the author

Bernie Dowling is an Australian writer working in journalism, fiction, and non-fiction.

His first novel is the neo-noir *Iraqi Icicle*. His non-fiction *Maaate! Bribe Proofing The Public Purse Against Good Blokes* is about corruption in local government.

From 2023-25, the author published a four-book series on film noir: *Noir Dirt Cheap*, Film *Noir Fate Vs The Working Stiff*, *Starry Starry Noir Rebels and Censors*, and *Three Faces of Noir Curse Crime Cringe*.

Man Of A Thousand Fails
Film Noir Of Elisha Cook Jr.

I didn't have the privilege of reading scripts. Guys called me up and said,
You're going to work tomorrow.
– Elisha Cook Jr.

Small in stature
Larger than Life
On the Big Screen

Introduction

In the unholy town of Hollywood, where the bottom line was the only scripture, Elisha Cook Jr. forged a career out of perpetual failure. His Biblical namesake was a prophet and miracle worker. The Hollywood Elisha was the patron saint of the broken and the doomed.

There are thousands of stories below the Hollywood sign. This is Elisha's.

For two decades, boyish Cook worked in vaudeville and theatre with bit parts in Hollywood comedies and musicals before audiences and producers noticed him. In films, he was uncredited and rarely made the posters. Then along came the Falcon.

Elisha Cook Jr. was 37 years old when *The Maltese Falcon* 1941 debuted. Cook played the gunsel, Wilmer Cook. A gunsel was a rent boy, usually a teenager, attached to a criminal. *The Maltese Falcon* author Dashiell Hammett did not clue his publisher about the meaning of the word. The publisher read it as gun toter. The censorious Hays Office banned "perverse" homosexuality from movies. It was obvious in Peter Lorre's character in *The Maltese Falcon*, but few viewers would have picked up on the acidic homophobia of Bogart's line:

"Keep that gunsel out of my way . . . I'll kill him."

Critics credit *The Maltese Falcon* as the first Hollywood film noir. Others say that tag belongs to the lesser-known *Stranger on the Third Floor* 1940 (with Cook, pictured above right). Cook and Peter Lorre appeared in both films. Both Cook's characters are losers. In *Stranger on the Third Floor*, Joe Briggs is on death row, after he is wrongly convicted of murder. Wilmer Cook in *The Maltese Falcon* is a psychopathic killer, vainly trying to mask his weak character.

The masked loser unmasked was the persona Cook performed with devastating effect in *The Big Sleep* 1946. He played Harry Jones, fatally attracted to the wrong woman who associated with vicious criminals. Losing in art imitated life when Cook's name failed to appear on movie posters for *The Maltese Falcon* and *The Big Sleep*.

Biting horror: Ketty Lester and Cook have fun in the blaxploitation movie *Blacula* 1972.
Lester was a successful singer in the 1950s and 1960s before she turned to film and television acting in the 1970s.

Cook's career in movies and television spanned six decades, but for many, his roles in film noir make him a much-loved actor, a man of a thousand fails, who has become immortal.

– Bernie Dowling, March 2026.

Chapter 1: A Life And Its Meanings

Film noir auteur and *The Maltese Falcon* director John Huston provided the best explanation of why Cook was a rare Hollywood bird whose carcass was unplucked by media and biographers.

Cook "lived alone up in the High Sierra, tied flies and caught golden trout between films. When he was wanted in Hollywood, they sent word up to his mountain cabin by courier. He would come down, do a picture, and then withdraw again to his retreat."
Huston, J. *An Open Book* 1994, Virgin Books London, page 79.

Pretty Kitty Blue Eyes 1944 was top-10 in the jukebox charts and was on the billboard charts for three months. Depending on how I framed the question that intrusive AI "informed" that the Merry Macs never recorded *Pretty Kitty Blue Eyes*, that they recorded it in 1937 (wrong) or they recorded it in 1944 (correct).

Being Hollywood lore, the Huston tale is embellished, but the kernel is solid truth. Cook, in 1928, married Mary Lou Cook, who later became a singer with the harmony quartet The Merry Macs. The couple divorced in 1941.

Peggy McKenna and Cook married in 1943, so his legendary mountain solitude was brief. But Cook did shun Hollywood glitz. He lived an outdoors lifestyle that included fly fishing.

What we do not know about Elisha Cook Jr. is more extensive than what we do. With more than 220 acting roles, he never had to run to the gossip journos to breathlessly tell his favorite color. He was born on December 26, 1903. Even his birth date marked him as the perennial loser with its celebration dove-tailing into Christmas.

Cook's name is not Christmasy, but it is religious themed. Elisha was an Israelite prophet. He was a miracle worker; a skill that film historian David Thomson wrote Cook brought to movies. "Put him in a bad picture, and he made it watchable for 10 minutes." (Thomson D, *The New Biographical Dictionary Of Film, Fourth Edition,* Alfred A. Knopf 2002, page 174).

Phantom Lady 1944 wasn't a bad picture, but it wasn't great except for the scene in which musician Cook simulates a sex act with his drum kit in a play for Ella Raines.

Cook was born into a theatrical family, though not a prominent one. Elisha Vanslyck Cook Sr. was a playwright and journalist. His wife Helen Roslyn Henry was an actor. As you would expect, the media, in covering the registry-office wedding, made more of the bride than the groom, noted only as the brother of Judge Carroll Cook of San Francisco. Helen Henry first appeared on the stage as an 11-year-old, twelve years before she married. The play was *A Celebrated Case* by Adolphe D'Ennery and Eugene Cormon. It opened in New York in 1878.
– *The San Francisco Examiner* Jul 24, 1900, p. 9.

Helen Henry was one Kevin-Bacon removed from fame of sorts when she performed with stock player Frank Bacon, the father of proto-noir director Lloyd Bacon (*Marked Woman* 1937, *San Quentin* 1937, and *Racket Busters* 1938). Frank Bacon struggled for years in repertory and vaudeville only to write, and star in the hit play *Lightnin'* in 1918. *Lightnin'* set the Broadway record of 1291 performances. Bacon starred in the first seven hundred when fatigue set in. He died of heart failure a week after his retirement in 1922. He was 58-years-old. Theater can be a tough game.

Shortly after their marriage, Elisha Sr. and Helen moved to Chicago, where Helen seems to have given up the stage, but Elisha Sr. wrote one-act plays and managed Little Theater companies. Cook Jr. graduated from selling programs and peanuts to stage management and acting in stock and vaudeville from age 14. Elisha Sr. died of pneumonia at the age of 54 in 1922. – *Chicago Tribune*, Dec 24, 1922, page 5.
Theater is a tough game.

At the time, Elisha Jr. was playing in the comedy *Thank-U* by Winchell Smith and Tom Cushing (styled *Thank You* on Broadway) at the Cort Theater. The lead was Edith King, who played in the 1946 noir *Calcutta*, starring Alan Ladd. The 1925 silent film *Thank You,* directed by John Ford, is lost.

Cook played in Chicago, toured, and eventually Broadway found him. For 18 years, he trod the boards with two film appearances in the lost film *Her Unborn Child* 1930, and the short Chills *and Fevers* 1930. Supporting performances in the latter, like Bogart's manners in *The Big Sleep* 1946, were pretty bad. It is a glee-club movie, aimed at the youth market. The star was Al Shean, uncle of the Marx Brothers and formerly half of the comedy duo Gallagher and Shean (1912-1914 and 1920-25). In 1922, the duo sang their song *Mr. Gallagher and Mr. Shean,* which performers mined for laughs for decades.

Cook's third film before his permanence in Hollywood was the drama *Honor Among Lovers* 1931. Cook was a bit player among main players who would make their marks in Hollywood – Claudette Colbert, Fredric March, Ginger Rogers, and Charles Ruggles.

Dorothy Arzner, lonesome as a woman director in Hollywood, directed. (The heydays of acclaimed silent director Lois Weber ended in 1923).

The acting in *Honor Among Lovers* is good, especially from Colbert. March and Ruggles are hindered by their characters, superficially affable but creepy. Arzner directs assuredly. But the script is slight and meanders between drama and spiteful comedy. At least we found out the rich staged lavish parties during which they played bridge and backgammon. That dissipated our envy of them as the Great Depression raged outside. Cook had only a fleeting part as an office boy.

His return to Hollywood five years later provided a much more substantial role on the back of Cook playing in Eugene O'Neill's hit play *Ah, Wilderness!* The comedy ran for two years on Broadway after opening at the Guild Theater in October 1933. Cook, 29, had the prime role of 16-year-old Richard Miller. The lead male was the Yankee Doodle Boy, George M. Cohan. In the cast was 10 year old Walter Vonnegut Jr., a cousin of future author Kurt Vonnegut Jr. Those Vonneguts sure saved on names. O'Neill himself selected Cook to play Richard, a partially autobiographical portrayal of the playwright as a youth. O'Neill must have sensed aspects of Cook's character that made him perfect for the role of Richard, the naïve revolutionary idealist. Unlike the short Cook, who had only three years of high school, tall young O'Neill headed to Yale, and he was a keen devourer of the plays of George Bernard Shaw and Oscar Wilde.

One reviewer who disparaged the play as unfunny found a hidden gem in "one of the loveliest of the theater's love scenes, made so in great measure by the sensitive, delicate and entirely fine performances of Elisha Cook Jr. and Ruth Gilbert, who play the roles."
– Burr E. *Billboard*, October 14, 1933.

Cook created his future film trope of a character who never received the good loving he craved. Ruth Gilbert continued to work on Broadway in the 1930s and 40s. She was in O'Neill's The *Iceman Cometh* 1946, and she replaced Lee Grant as a shoplifter in the play *Detective Story*. Female *Ah, Wilderness!* Lead Adelaide Bean was later blacklisted from television, rarer than a ban from films. Resolute Bean went back to the theater.

Anyone watching *Two in a Crowd* 1936 saw Elisha Cook Jr, was third lead. Yet his name appeared on the poster in small print with an "e" added to Cook.

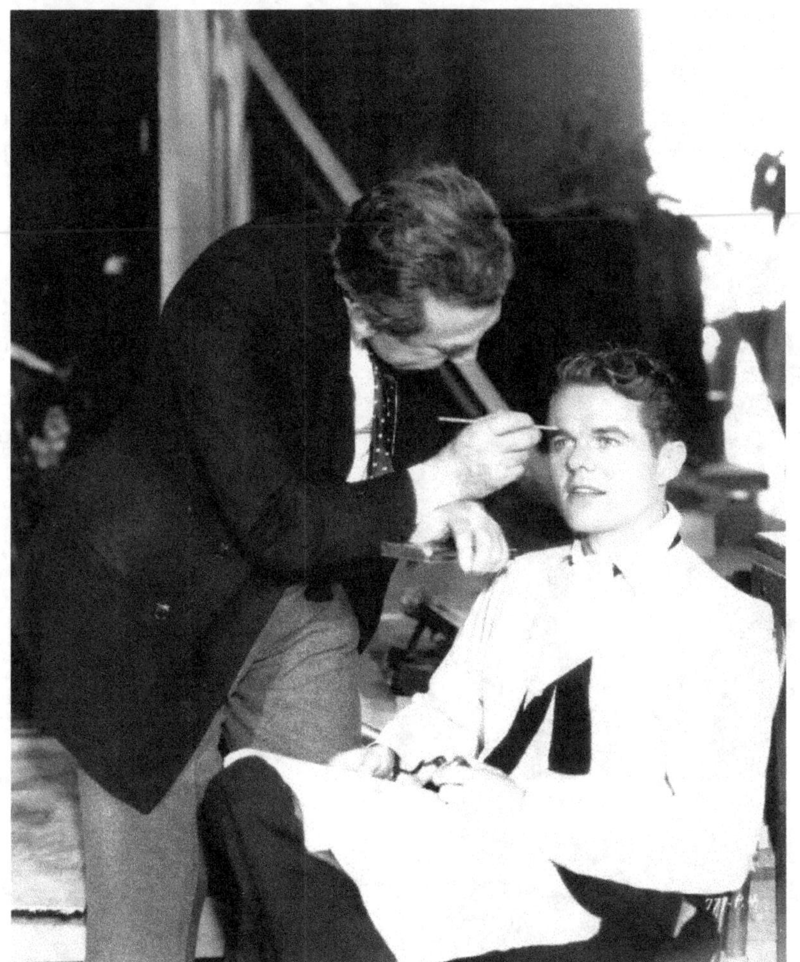

Making up for scarce roles: Austrian-American actor Otto Lederer moved into makeup in the 1930s. He applied the craft to Cook for *Two in a Crowd*. The film featured horse racing. Cook has in his lap either the script or a racing form guide.

What irked the cinema gods about Cook that, for much of his career, they deleted him from movie and poster credits? At least it fitted with his repeated character role of the loser.

Two in a Crowd was a screwball comedy, a genre named after a baseball pitch with reverse spin. Elements of screwball comedy included eccentric characters, slapstick, fast-paced humor, and satire. An eccentric character appears in the third act. In the world of screwball, clever women often overcame stuffed-shirt men. Female lead was blonde Joan Bennett – notice the top billing – who went on to dye her hair brunette to become a noir icon in films such as *The Woman in the Window* 1944, *Scarlet Street* 1945, *The Woman on the Beach* 1947, and The *Reckless Moment* 1949.

Cook played a jockey. His horse could only win when annoyed by something, a business copied by the Marx Brothers in the next year's *A Day at the Races* 1937. In *Two in a Crowd* Cook had adequate screen time to provide a fine entrée to his lengthy career in film.

Chapter 2: The movies

Elisha Cook Jr. appeared in more than 120 films, screened in cinemas and on television, over almost 60 years from 1930 to 1987. Another one hundred roles were in television and drama. Between the designated film-noir years, 1940-59, Cook appeared in twenty noirs.

His sole starring role during this time was in the 30-min army training film, *Baptism of Fire* 1943.

In a show of patriotism, Hollywood nominated it for best documentary though it was a fictional drama, preparing recruits for combat stress.

Cook's role as level-headed soldier Bill was uncredited. Omission from credits was a feature of his career.

Noir stylistics migrated to television in the 1950s and Cook went with them. A 1953 episode of *The Adventures of Superman* (1952-58) was *Semi-Private Eye* in which Cook played a PI. The ep was a vehicle for Jack Larson (Jimmy Olsen) to impersonate Humphrey Bogart in his noir roles.

Bogart overcame typecasting in crime movies, but Larson made only irregular television roles after playing cub reporter Jimmy. He branched out into production and creating musicals as a librettist.

Cook's TV roles included *Alfred Hitchcock Presents* 1955, *Perry Mason* 1958, *Rawhide* 1959, *Peter Gunn* 1960, *Tightrope!* 1960, and *Thriller* 1960, hosted by Boris Karloff.

Cook was a reliable sparkler added to the repetitive fireworks of monochrome television, but he shone as a bit player in classic noir:

They Won't Forget, a 1937 proto-noir.

Danger – Love at Work, a 1937 screwball comedy directed by noir auteur Otto Preminger (*Laura* 1944, *Fallen Angel* 1945, *Where the Sidewalk Ends* 1950, *The Man with the Golden Arm* 1955, and *Anatomy of a Murder* 1959).

Stranger on the Third Floor 1940.

The Maltese Falcon 1941.

I Wake Up Screaming 1941.

Phantom Lady 1944.

Dark Mountain 1944.

Dark Waters 1944.

Blonde Alibi 1946.

The Falcon's Alibi 1946 with Jane Greer, who was the iconic femme fatale Kathie Moffat in *Out of the Past* 1947.

The Big Sleep 1946.

Fall Guy 1947.

Born To Kill 1947.

The Long Night 1947.

The Gangster 1947.

Flaxy Martin 1949.

Don't Bother to Knock 1952.

I, the Jury 1953.

The Killing 1956.

Accused of Murder 1956.

Voodoo Island 1957 horror film, director Reginald LeBorg (*Destiny* 1944, Fall Guy 1947) and starring Boris Karloff (*Frankenstein* 1931, *Targets* 1968).

Chicago Confidential 1957.

Plunder Road 1957.

Baby Face Nelson 1957.

The Outfit 1973 neo-noir.

Hammett 1982 neo-noir.

The Man Who Broke 1,000 Chains 1987.

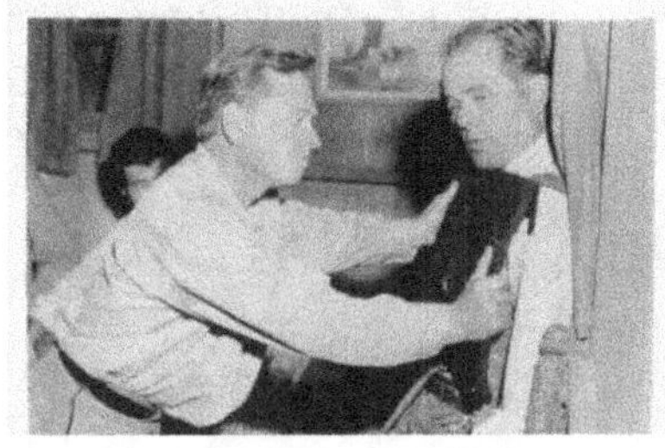

Die once again: *Baby Face Nelson*

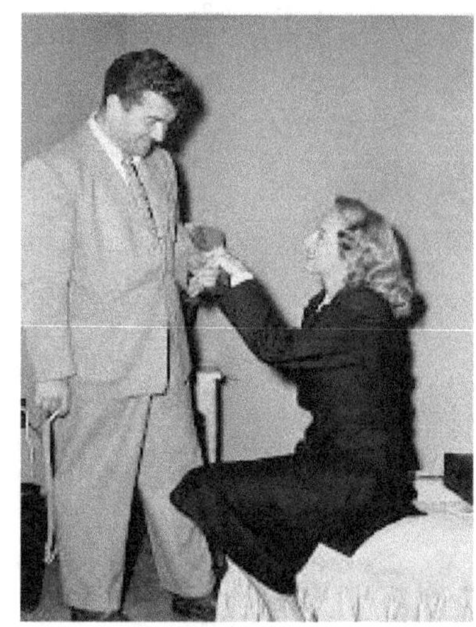

Bug-eyed Big-noter:
In the excellent 1937 proto-noir *They Won't Forget*, Cook plays a teenager going steady with Lana Turner who is murdered on Confederate Memorial Day.

He basks in the publicity but, in court, he is unable to say whether he kissed Lana. Come on, Elisha, you couldn't get within the same postcode as Lana Turner.

Noir polymath Robert Rossen wrote the screenplay for *They Will Not Forget*, along with Aben Kandel. Rossen had the knack of combining personal drama with political analysis in such noirs as *Out of the Fog* 1941, *The Stange Love of Martha Ivers* 1946, *Desert Fury* 1947, *Body and Soul* 1947 (as director), *All the King's Men* 1949 (as writer/ director/ producer), and the neo-noir *The Hustler* 1961 (as writer/ director/ producer). After blacklisting for two years, Rossen named fifty-seven former communists and supporters to the House Un-American Activities Committee (HUAC). He died aged fifty-seven.

Noir icons: Rossen and Evelyn Keyes. The movie was *Johnny O'Clock* 1947. Rossen wrote and directed but it was not among his best work.

The movie starts with Dixie music, a statue of Abraham Lincoln and another of General Robert E. Lee, with the inscription:

All the South ever desired was the Union, as established by our Forefathers, should be preserved.

Was Lee referring to a pre-Civil War Union with slavery? The title *They Won't Forget* has a veiled meaning. "Lest We Forget" is a standard war-memorial phrase and the annual parade, led by six remaining Confederate veterans in their nineties, is the background to the action. What they also will not forget is animosity between North and South, lingering 70 years after the war's end. Or one hundred years after, as shown by the Band's 1969 song *The Night They Drove Old Dixie Down*, written by Robbie Robertson. Or 160 years later with current hostility created by the removal of Confederate iconography and place names.

Teenager Lana Turner (*The Postman Always Rings Twice* 1946) is murdered. Politically ambitious DA Claude Rains (*Moontide* 1942, *Casablanca* 1942, *Notorious* 1946, *The Unsuspected* 1947) wants to leverage into high office the conviction of a Northerner. Northern newspapers print stories claiming unjustified southern prejudice.

The story is based on the lynching of Leo Frank in 1913, an act of antisemitism rather than prejudice against a Northerner. In *Crossfire* 1947, the motive for murder changed to antisemitism from the homophobia in Richard Brooks' source novel. Hollywood is a weird town. The change to North-South conflict works well in the film.

The Verdict: *They Won't Forget* 

In Cook's next film *Danger – Love at Work* 1937, he does a bit of business with screwball-comedy stuffed-shirt Edward Everett Horton, pictured with the lantern at right. In their interchange, Cook and Horton satirize self-improvement shysters operating during the Great Depression.

What interests noiristas about this film are its connections of cast and crew to noir classics. The director was Otto Preminger: *Laura* 1944, *Fallen Angel* 1945, *Where the Sidewalk Ends* 1950, *The Man with the Golden Arm 1955*, and *Anatomy of a Murder*, 1959. Lead Ann Sothern stepped away from comedy for the noirs *Shadow on the Wall* 1950 and Fritz Lang's *The Blue Gardenia* 1953. I burst into smiles at the *Danger – Love at Work* scenes featuring dire noir performer John Carradine (*Swamp Water* 1941, *Bluebeard* 1944, and *Fallen Angel* 1945). Carradine was not outrageously funny as an eccentric artist, but it struck me as absurd to have him in such a role.

Preminger's direction is proficient, and the ensemble cast professional. The good-natured film entices the audience to wish it to take off, but it never does. It was not Otto Preminger's métier. But I will always be grateful for these lines, spoken by the eccentric scientist with a genius for a pre-teen son. "Junior won't let me have the Nobel Prize. I don't think that's fair, do you? Just because he's the youngest prodigy ever to enter Harvard." The logic is strained, but the childish adult reminds me of someone.

The Verdict: *Danger – Love at Work* 

Critics and academics divide on whether *The Maltese Falcon* 1941 or *Stranger on the Third Floor* 1940 was the first Hollywood noir. Whichever you favor, actors Elisha Cook Jr. and Peter Lorre had the distinction of being in both. For me, Stranger is a noir and preceded the Falcon, so I am in the corner of the earlier film as the first noir.

French film critic Nino Frank coined the label "film noir" (dark film) when he discussed four American films, only available in France after World War II that ended in 1945. The films were *The Maltese Falcon, Laura* 1944, *Murder, My Sweet* 1944, and *Double Indemnity* 1944. I can only presume Frank missed *Stranger on the Third Floor* 1940 or he would have included that one.

By now you will not be surprised that Cook failed to make the opening credits for *Stranger on the Third Floor* . But RKO was kind enough to provide an extended list of the main players, that placed Cook as fifth lead.

I miss that quaint practice that sometimes extended to providing images of the players in character. It might look oddly quaint for a film today, but it would please us strange nostalgists.

I suspect producer Lee Marcus (proto-noir *Full Confession* 1939) had an eye to Lorre's startling performance in Fritz Lang's *M* 1931 in casting *Stranger on the Third Floor*.

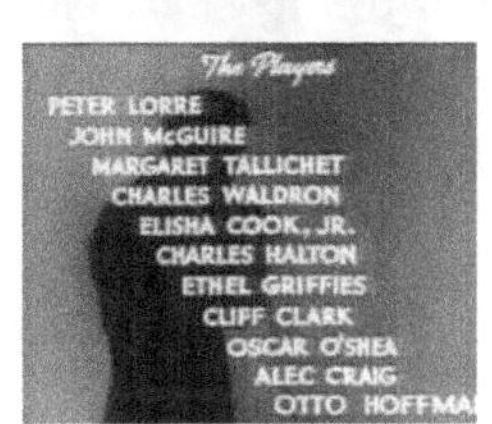

Stranger on the Third Floor has a run-time of a tick over 60mins. People count this as negative, but I am fond of a good one-hr. movie and a good 2-min pop song (*The Letter* 1968 by the Box Tops comes in at 1:58 and is a favorite).

It is amusing that contemporary critics derided that first film noir as derivative. It paid homage to German Expressionism as director Boris Ingster was a Russian expat and writer Frank Partos hailed from Hungary, as did lead Peter Lorre. Cinematographer Nicholas Musuraca was from Italy. While Expressionist techniques were in Hollywood horror and gangster films from the second half of the 1920s, the crew of *Stranger on the Third Floor* were among the first, along with Director Fritz Lang (*Fury* 1936) to assiduously apply them to crime films evolving during the second half of the 1930s.

The movie starts cleverly. A middle-class couple plan marriage and renting an apartment. It's a classic Hitchcockian bait and switch. Grim events will intrude. Margaret Tallichet looks at a newspaper story showing her partner John McQuire as a key witness to a murder. "I didn't know he (the accused) was so young. He looks like a kid," Ms. Tallichet says. Don't we just know she is talking about Elisha Cook Jr., 37 years young?

Cook gives a reliable performance as the frightened man facing the death penalty on circumstantial evidence. He understandably lied to police about a previous robbery conviction, and this is working against him.

The yummy set design by Van Nest Polglase (*Citizen Kane* 1941, *Suspicion* 1941, and *Gilda* 1946) is enhanced by the moody photography of Nicholas Musuraca (*The Spiral Staircase* 1946, *Deadline at Dawn* 1946, *Out of the Past* 1947, *Clash by Night* 1952, *The Hitch-Hiker* 1953, and *The Blue Gardenia* 1953.

Stranger on the Third Floor Screenwriter Frank Partos wrote noirs *The Snake Pit* 1948, and *The House on Telegraph Hill* 1951.

Polymath: *Stranger on the Third Floor* director Boris Ingster is not mentioned in David Thomson's comprehensive biographical dictionary of film. This is a little surprising as the born and raised Latvian was a noteworthy if not prolific writer, producer, and director in Hollywood.

The other noir he directed was the documentary-styled *Southside 1-1000* 1950. If you survive the introductory eulogy of the arms dealer and the dollar, it is watchable.

In co-writing the a-historic *The Last Days of Pompeii* 1935, Ingster, the former ally of Soviet film-maker Sergei Eisenstein, weaves in metaphors of working-class deprivations.

Abetted by savage satirical novelist Nathanael West (*The Day of the Locust* 1939) as co-writer, Frank Partos shows the injustice of the justice system trying Cook. A bailiff must wake the sleeping judge to admonish a sleeping juror. In another scene, a strenuous objection from Cook's appointed defence attorney awakens the judge, who decides to sustain the objection he has not heard. This low-budget noir packs a lot into its 60 minutes.

Be honest, how many names in the cast do you recognize besides Cook and Lorre? Double points if you say Margaret Tallichet and add that she was married to director William Wyler for 42 years. The point is that cast members were unknowns who performed well. Thus, the *M*-man Lorre received top billing though he had 10 minutes of screen time. And what a riveting 10-minutes they were. Knowing that readers will not have seen this under-appreciated noir classic, I will refrain from further discussion of the plot.

The verdict: *Stranger on the Third Floor.* ★★★★⯪

Chapter 5: The Day of the Falcon

The influence of *The Maltese Falcon* on film careers is extraordinary. The bankability of the silent star Mary Astor, who plays Brigid O'Shaughnessy, returned from hibernation. Peter Lorre recovered from playing the stock character of Japanese soldier of fortune Mr. Moto in the low-budget series of films from 1937-39. Humphrey Bogart, regarded by Warners as a perennial B-lister, had turned forty and soared from type-casting as the gangster villain. Screenwriter John Huston achieved well beyond the expectations of Warners' studio execs who had made good on a promise to give Huston a crack at directing. Obese theater actor, sexagenarian Sydney Greenstreet, turned his first film role into an Oscar nomination and a decade of memorable performances in noirs. Ward Bond had been a support in good films, but the Falcon propelled him into more prominent roles in association with John Wayne and John Ford. And Elisha Cook Jr. nailed the character of a man yearning for respect but weighed down by personality flaws that turn the dream into a nightmare. He ran with it in a string of noirs, without distraction from Hollywood fanfare and glamor.

John Huston described the exhilaration engendered on the set of *The Maltese Falcon* when the ensemble realized they were creating something special. "We were all having such a good time together on *Falcon* that, night after night after night, after shooting, Bogie, Peter Lorre, Ward Bond, Mary Astor and I would go over to the Lakeside Country Club. We'd have a few drinks, then a buffet supper, and stay on till midnight. We all thought we were doing something good, but no one had any idea *The Maltese Falcon* would be a great success and eventually take its place as a film classic."
Huston, J. *An Open Book* 1994, Virgin Books, London, page 79.
Cook and the Falcon's senior partner Greenstreet were absentees from the nights of celebration. It was typical of Cook's work/ home balance and not a sign that he was less enthusiastic about the movie than the others. He always cited it as his favorite film. "There wasn't one decent person in the whole film," he said approvingly.
– *Variety* May 29, 1995, obituary.

While Cook's assessment might not be totally true, it indicated how the four crooks – Greenstreet, Astor, Lorre, and Cook – spiced up the movie. Once you have watched the Falcon half a dozen times, advisable for any noir lover, what always brings a smile is this exchange between Bogie and his secretary, played by Lee Patrick (who had a memorable support role in *The Snake Pit* 1948).

Bogie: What's your woman's intuition tell you about her (O'Shaughnessy)?
Patrick: She's alright, if that's what you mean?
Bogie: That's what I mean.

The softly spoken breathy fabulist with witty self-deprecation, O'Shaughnessy, is so convincing that she fools Patrick and makes a sceptical Bogart fall in love with her. The joy of watching the Falcon repeatedly is your ability to devour the delicate acting of the six principals (seven when you count Ward Bond, who plays a sympathetic but frustrated police detective.

Lorre introduces himself as a polite but determined thief who signals his sexuality with gardenia perfume. Bogart easily subdues Lorre as he does with the other short man, the psychopathic Cook.

Director Huston knew what presence the massive Greenstreet would bring to the film, so his name is repeated before his entrance. The ploy is so effective that the moniker Gutman sounds sinister rather than cartoonish. "The Fatman, is he here?" Gutman is Goodman in Yiddish and German, adding another humorous twist to the character's name.

As I have said, Greenstreet was nominated for best male support at the 14th Academy Awards. Englishman Donald Crisp won for his part in the rural drama *How Green Was My Valley*, directed by John Ford, and set in Wales. John Huston was nominated for best adapted screenplay, won by Sidney Buchman and Seton I. Miller for the fantasy romcom *Here Comes Mr. Jordan*. Mary Astor won best female support, but it was for another villainous role in *The Great Lie* 1941. Astor was not nominated for best female actor, won by Joan Fontaine for *Suspicion* 1941, directed by Alfred Hitchcock.

Greenstreet, Bogart, and Lorre reunited in the romantic adventure *Casablanca* 1942. Lorre and Bogart had this immortal sharp exchange.

Lorre: You despise me, don't you?

Bogart: Well, if I gave you any thought, I probably would.

First edition: The original cover is at left.

Fight: O'Shaughnessy assaults Cairo, below.

Those familiar with the title *The Maltese Falcon* may be acquainted with the movie rather than Dashiell Hammett's 1930 novel, published by Alfred A. Knopf. There is a remarkable constructive interaction between novel and film, without parallel in such translations. Writer/ director John Huston wrote the script to closely follow the order of the novel, retained much of the dialogue, and then filmed it in sequence. He rehearsed extensively to achieve the precise timing that elevates the dialog.

Cairo: "Shall we add more certainty, the boy outside?"

O'Shaughnessy: "You might be able to get around him, Joel, like you did the one in Istanbul. What was his name?"

Cairo: "You mean the one you couldn't get to . . ."

Huston persuaded censors to let him keep the recurring motif of hard liquor. No censor objected to the continual prop of cigarettes. Huston self-censored to remove most of the key homosexual references in the novel, but the character of Joel would have had sophisticated viewers clearly seeing the elephant in the room.

Readers are often disconsolate when a favourite novel is translated onto the screen. In this case, the film enhances a re-read of the novel as the reader can have the authentic dialogue, voiced in their mind by Bogart, Greenstreet, Lorre, Astor, Gladys George (widow of Miles Archer, Bogie's murdered partner) Cook, Patrick, and Bond.

Although neither was a prolific writer, Hammett and Raymond Chandler (*The Big Sleep* 1939, *Farewell, My Lovely* 1940, *The High Window* 1942, *The Lady in the Lake* 1943) after him, were among the inventors of the hard-boiled detective novels that morphed into 1940s film noir.

Hammett, left.

Chandler, right.

Both authors have been recognised as great writers, not just as doyens of their genre. I do not believe any of the current crop of superstars of the detective thriller will garner such recognition in the future. In 1998, the Modern Library ranked *The Maltese Falcon* 56th on its list of the one hundred best English-language novels of the 20th century.

Hammett and Chandler had similar histories before their emergence as writers of edgy fiction. In World War I, both suffered debilitating injuries, the effects of which remained all their lives. They reached the peaks of their writing careers during the 1930s Great Depression that followed the decade of post-war license hailed as the Roaring Twenties.

The plot of *The Maltese Falcon* evolves from the murder of private detective Miles Archer, business partner of the protagonist Samuel Spade. The story is written in the third person with no interior monologue, yet the reader identifies with the character of flawed Spade.

What makes this novel good are the sparse style and the clipped dialogue – tougher than Chandler's, though not as funny.

The author uses detailed character descriptions and dialogue to render the story without any back-up of interior reflection or self-justification. Spade's moral ambiguity is a magnificent device upon which to pin suspense. As Gutman says of Spade, we never know what he is going to do or say next.

The reader learns early on that Spade has been having an emotionless sexual affair with his dead partner's wife, Iva. The shamus grumbles to his loyal secretary, Effie Perine, 'I never know what to do or say to women except that way.' That line, as good as it is, was omitted from the movie. The Hays Office censors or John Huston felt that PI Sam Spade's promiscuity should not be stressed but referred to coyly.

Homosexuality is central to the novel though it does not have as many echoes of homophobia as it often does with Chandler.

Let's start with the least clear-cut example. Secretary Effie Perine lives at home with her mother. Effie appears to have a woman crush on femme fatale Brigid O'Shaughnessy, who, in the manner of the heterosexual genre, must be Spade's love interest.

The hint at lesbianism is subtle and possibly unintended but look for the fascinating reactions of Perine in the last pages of the novel, if you decide to read or re-read it.

Joel Cairo is obviously homosexual as delightfully rendered by the gardenia perfume, the cane he puts to his lips, and his exchange with the promiscuous O'Shaughnessy that results in her assaulting him.

The sinister urbane Gutman has a daughter (important in the novel but left out of the movie), but he is bisexual. The psychotic young gunman Wilmer Cook is referred to in the novel as "the boy" as he is in various parts of the film. The insinuation, strong in the novel, and weaker in the film, is that Wilmer Cook is Gutman's kept boy. Wilmer's bisexuality creates a powerful sub-plot in the novel.

The Maltese Falcon first appeared serialised in the pulp fiction mag *Black Mask*. Magazine editor Joseph Shaw recoiled from the vulgarity, but he liked the word gunsel (also gunzel). In fact, the editor loved its use in the novel.

Shaw thought gunsel meant hired gun and a host of Hammett imitators used it in that sense. You will still see that meaning in dictionaries. Gunsel meant a boy or young man paid or kept for sex, a rent boy, especially one attached to a criminal.

Climbing a mountain to the top:

The path to the Falcon's success was paved by the release of a modest gangster film earlier that year of 1941. Raoul Walsh (*The Roaring Twenties* 1939, *They Drive by Night* 1940) was the director and John Huston, the scriptwriter, along with W.R. Burnett, author of the source novel.

Huston said, "Paul Muni was offered the lead, and I was pleased when he turned it down turned it down and Humphrey Bogart got to do it. Before this picture Bogie was well down the list at Warners."

– Huston J. 1994, page 78.

With the success of *High Sierra*, Huston chose Hammett's novel to fulfil the bargain with Warners that he could direct. Warners still had the option on the Falcon that they had turned into other versions. *The Maltese Falcon* 1931 recreated only snatches of Hammett while *Satan Met a Lady* 1935, a better movie, wildly diverged from the novel and its title had no relevance to the book. Producers were surprised when the neophyte director went for a third drink at the well. Huston said, "*Falcon* had never really been put on the screen." – Huston J. 1994, page 78.

Just as Bogart got his chance at *High Sierra* by Muni passing, George Raft rejected the offer of the Falcon lead, and Huston was pleased that Bogie got the shot.

What is it with marketing people? Huston, the players, and crew reproduced an authentic Hammett. Warners publicity wanted to call it *The Gent from Frisco*. That sounds like a Damon Runyon comedy. And there are no gents in the Falcon. Not even close. Warners head of production, Hal Wallis, who surprised by turning up at the preview along with studio head Jack Warner, vetoed the change of title.

To capitalize on the unexpected success of the Falcon, Huston directed the war adventure *Across the Pacific* 1942 with Bogart, Astor, and Greenstreet in the leads. Also, the cinematographer was Arthur Edeson (*The Maltese Falcon, Casablanca* (1942, directed by Michael Curtiz). *Across the Pacific* was quite profitable for Warners but has not achieved the legendary status of *The Maltese Falcon* and *Casablanca*.

Wilmer Cook, Elisha's gunsel character in the Falcon, talks tough, but Spade continually humiliates him. Cook is good with threats: "Keep asking for it and you're gonna get it. Plenty." But it is Cook whom Bogart disarms and roughs up. Cook is a remorseless killer, but we imagine he ambushed his victims. In one scene Spade hands Gutman two of Wilmer's guns, "A crippled newsie took 'em away from him. I made him give 'em back." The amoral Gutman agrees to give up his young lover to the police. "Well, Wilmer, I'm sorry indeed to lose you. But I want you to know I couldn't be fonder of you if you were my own son. But, well, if you lose a son, it's possible to get another. There's only one Maltese Falcon." Tough guy Wilmer is a loser.

The eyes have it:

Like other proficient character actors, Elisha Cook Jr. had great control over his facial expressions. In this scene from *The Maltese Falcon*, Wilmer knows the gig is up and becomes a frightened little boy.

In an earlier scene, when he pretends he is not following Spade, he has a blank expression when confronted.

We'll always have *Casablanca*: Arthur Edeson shoots Bogie and Bergman.

Cinematographers operating on B-movies, free of studio supervision, were part of the artistic success stories of noir. Falcon cinematographer Arthur Edeson had a storied career before and after the 1941 film. Edeson began his lengthy career in 1914. One of his early films of interest is the comedy *In Again, Out Again* 1917 starring Douglas Fairbanks and Arline Pretty, with a screenplay by Anita Loos, author of the novella *Gentlemen Prefer Blondes* 1925, translated into the 1928 and 1953 films. Edeson shot the spectacular adventures, *The Thief of Bagdad* 1924 and *The Lost World* 1925 before the talkie *All Quiet on the Western Front* 1930 that won best film and best director (Lewis Milestone) at the 3rd Academy Awards. Edeson was nominated for best cinematography. His other nominations were for *In Old Arizona* 1928 and *Casablanca*.

Edeson acknowledged the influence of German Expressionism on his work, which included *Frankenstein* 1931, *They Drive by Night* 1940, *The Mask of Dimitrios* 1944, *Nobody Lives Forever* 1946, and *Three Strangers* 1946.

The signals of noir:

Notice the noir motifs captured in the Falcon. At top we have the light and shade, chiaroscuro. Above is light and shade within askew walls and a distant light signalling the forlorn remoteness of peace. Spade is on the phone at right with faded vertical and horizontal lines at askew angles behind him.

Wilted flowers are a deft touch.

They work by night. Film editors are the most anonymous of cinematic creatives. Sure, they get Academy Awards, but what winners and their films can you name? Remember William Holden's line from the noir satire *Sunset Boulevard* 1950, "Audiences don't know somebody sits down and writes a picture; they think the actors make it up as they go along. Editors could make a similar lament, "They think movies come out of the camera that way." Thomas Richards was the editor of *The Maltese Falcon,* and *They Drive by Night* 1940. In the driver's seat above is alert George Raft with nervous passengers Bogie and Ann Sheridan.

After leaping from scriptwriting to directing, John Huston realized the interdependence of photography, directing, composition, and editing.

"You've got to figure out how each shot is to be coordinated with all the other shots that will ultimately make up the sequence, even though the individual, intercut shots may be photographed days apart." Huston J. *American Cinematographer* Dec. 1941.

In *The Maltese Falcon*, the rare practice of shooting the scenes in order, and cutting little of the dialogue, assisted in providing the basis for clean editing and a movie easy for audiences to follow, not always the case in noir.

Films Thomas Richards edited include the proto-noir *Each Dawn I Die* 1939, *Castle on the Hudson* 1940, *It All Came True* 1940, *Flight from Destiny* 1941, and *The Seventh Cross* 1944.

The verdict:
The Maltese Falcon ★★★★★

Don't hurt me: Victor Mature roughs up apartment concierge Cook.

Bogart parlayed leads in *High Sierra* and The Maltese Falcon into becoming the top noir star over the next fifteen years. The fortunes of a character actor such as Cook were at the whim of producers and casting despite his impressive bit parts in Stranger and the Falcon. Fortunately, he was selected for another winner after the Falcon. *I Wake Up Screaming* 1941 was a noir that did good box office.

Again, Cook's name was excluded from opening credits and posters. Alan Mowbray and Allyn Joslyn who made opening creds and posters were hardly household names. British actor Mowbray had been playing bit parts in Hollywood for a dozen years and his seniority won a place in publicity.

Cook's anonymity in pre-publicity was a feature of his storied career. I have no evidence, but I wonder if Cook and his agent figured humility in refusing credits might enhance his value as a character actor. We do know the playwright, Owen Davis, gave him this advice when Cook left for Hollywood,

"Junior, if you want to be intelligent, play small parts, because then they can never blame you if the movie is bad."

Yearsley, D. *Anderson Valley Advertiser*, May 24, 1995.

The producers of *I Wake Up Screaming* were astute to give Cook, another bland name, this time Harry Wliiams. We meet Harry when he disses one of the apartment tenants, "hash slinger" Vicky Lynn (Carole Landis) who unbeknown to Williams is being promoted to be a star by publicist Frankie Christopher (Victor Mature) who teaches frightened Harry to show respect.

As I said, it was a popular B-picture from Warners who wanted to extend the range of Betty Grable from comedies and musicals. But, like Sam Spade's character, the film was flawed. After the police interrogation that tells us it is a noir and a mystery, it lifts part of the plot of George Bernard Shaw's *Pygmalion* (translated to later stage and screen as *My Fair Lady*). Mature bets two pals, Mowbray and Joslyn, he can turn waiter Landis into a star.

Multiple flashbacks telling the story of a murder work well. The better noir *Laura* 1944 replicated this style.

Shooter:
I Wake Up Screaming's experienced shooter Edward Cronjager (*Desert Fury* 1947, *House by the River* 1950) delivers striking images.

Unfortunately, much dialogue does not ring true. Grable says to her sister, "What you need now is sleep; if you lose your looks, you've lost your entire bankroll." Mature threatens huge police detective Laird Cregar, "If I ever find you around here again, they will have to pick you up with a sieve." He later refers to Cregar as *Operator 13*, the title character played by Marion Davies in the 1934 romance film about a Yankee spy in the Confederate South.

Elisha Cook Jr. was 38 years old in 1941 but referred to in the movie as "a boy by the name of Harry Williams". Cook has a doleful look on his face when he says he wanted to go to murder-victim Vicky's funeral. Grable asks him why he did not, and he replies. "I didn't think it was my place." As in many a role, Cook was pathetic in both the literal and colloquial sense of the word.

Laird Cregar as vengeful, psychotic, police detective Ed Cornell steals the movie. Cinematographer Edward Cronjager shoots Cregar from unflattering angles and half-hidden in shadows. He is like *Cape Fear*'s Max Cady, only more frightening because Ed Cornell wears a badge.

After his success in Screaming, obese Cregar shed weight to star in the Jack-the-Ripper noir *The Lodger* 1944 and another noir set in London, *Hangover Square* 1945. Cregar died from a heart attack before the release of the latter film. He was 31 years old.

Aged twenty-nine, Carole Landis suicided after a relationship with a married man. You can research the details if you wish.

Betty Grable, a heavy smoker all her adult life, though rarely in movies, died, aged fifty-six, from lung cancer, in 1973.

Grable was competent but not outstanding in the role of a shy woman determined to find her sister's murderer. She falls for Mature which we knew would happen, but she cannot shake the possibility he could be the killer. Grable was not confident in her ability to pull off the dramatic roles Warners wanted for her. In 1942 she told Life Magazine, "There are two reasons why I became a star, and I'm standing on both of them." This was a line in a multiple-page spread concentrating on Grable's famed legs. I suspect publicity or a journalist made up the leggy quote for Grable, but that just cynical ol' me.

I Wake Up Screaming includes a swimming scene to show off Grable's legs and Mature's buff torso. It was equal-opportunity sexploitation. The idea of going to a pool popped into beefcake Mature's head. But where did they get the swimwear?

In 1943, Betty Grable's legs were insured for $1million. If you cynically say it sounds like a publicity stunt, you are on the money. Studio 20th Century Fox did the insuring. In 1952, the legs of dancer/actor Cyd Charise were insured for $5 million, well, you know, inflation. This time MGM did the insuring, proving again that the only 'ism" Hollywood believes in is plagiarism. (The plagiarism witticism is attributed to Dorothy Parker, but I like to think she took it from someone else, thus affirming the veracity of the bon mot. I could have reaffirmed it myself by claiming credit for it, rather than mentioning Ms. Parker).

It is 53 minutes into *I Wake Up Screaming* that Grable and Mature kiss, and that horrid man, Mr. Cregar, interrupts the passion. Grabbing an incriminating letter, he says to Mature, "I knew you were holding something back. You're the Mona Lisa type. I can spot 'em a mile away".

Scriptwriter Dwight Taylor piled on the cryptic metaphors. He outdid himself when Cregar asks the DA, "Have you read *The Sex Life of the Butterfly* by Faber?" The book did not exist. That did not stop Taylor from creating a preposterous tale of what was in it.

Elisha Cook Jr. is in only three scenes in *I Wake Up Screaming*, but he makes each count, with expressive physical and facial moves. The three scenes occur in the beginning, middle, and end of the movie. They surprisingly link, though that probably escaped most viewers. Again, Cook gave a polished professional performance as a scared little man with dreams beyond his social skills.

The verdict: *I Wake Up Screaming* 
Add a star or two if you love weirdness.

Chapter 7: Phantom sex

Mention *Phantom Lady* 1944 and anyone who has seen it pictures drummer Elisha Cook Jr. simulating a sex act with his kit. The producers knew it would pack a wallop, and they felt they needed to include Cook in the opening credits. Not on the first grab that was reserved for Tone, Raines, and Curtis. As sixth lead, no "e" on Cook, but a pedant might quibble about the comma between Cook and Jr.

Let us dwell on names. Established star Tone took roles in film noir and crime – the proto-noir *They Gave Him a Gun* 1937, *Five Graves to Cairo* 1943, and *Dark Waters* 1944.

Young Raines starred in *Phantom Lady*, her third movie, and her first noir. She went on to the noirs, *Time Out of Mind* 1947 (a flop), *The Suspect* 1944 (a good Edwardian period crime drama), *The Strange Affair of Uncle Harry* 1945, *The Web* 1947, *Brute Force* 1947, *Impact* 1949, and *A Dangerous Profession* 1949 (such as making loss-inducing noirs).

Who was *Phantom Lady* third-billed Alan Curtis, I hear you ask.

Curtis had small roles until the noir *High Sierra* 1941, in which he was third lead.

He had the lead as composer Franz Schubert in *The Great Awakening* 1941 and was male lead in the wonderfully titled war noir *Hitler's Madman* 1943. He was in the noir *Inside Job* 1946, and he played sleuth Philo Vance in two films.

The reason he is not remembered may be because of his death after routine surgery in 1953. He was 43 years old. Chain smoker Franchot Tone, 63, died of lung cancer in 1968.

Fourth lead Spanish-American actor Thomas Gomez was a late-comer to films in 1942 after twenty years on the stage. He was nominated for an Oscar for his role in the underrated noir *Ride the Pink Horse* 1947. He appeared in *A Double Life* 1947, *Key Largo* 1948, and *Force of Evil* 1948.

Sistas: Aurora Miranda, left, and Carmen Miranda, below.

Aurora Miranda, billed as Aurora in *Phantom Lady* was the younger sister of Carmen, famous for her fruity, flowery, and other unusual headwear. Aurora plays a nightclub singer who has an assortment of headwear. I am not sure whether the sisters' penchant for alluring hats was the inspiration for the movies throughline about hats. It was the sort of inspiration best left unindulged.

And that is the basic problem with *Phantom Lady* which privileges style over substance. As a thriller it is sloppy, lingering over impressive scenes created by director Robert Siodmak, bound for noir glory, once he controlled his arthouse vibes. Later noirs included *The Suspect* 1944, *The Spiral Staircase* 1945, *The Killers* 1946, *The Dark Mirror* 1946, the excellent *Criss Cross* 1949, and *The File on Thelma Jordon* 1949.

The director

Robert Siodmak was born in Germany in 1900. He got a start in movies in the mid-1920s when American-born producer Seymour Nebenzal, working in Germany, hired him to create new movies from bits of old stock. In a way, Siodmak was a pioneer of AI without the computer.

Siodmak's first original film was the silent drama *People on Sunday* 1929, co-written by Billy Wilder. Noir icons Edgar G. Ulmer and Fred Zinnemann assisted Siodmak.

38

Siodmak left Germany for France in 1933 when Hitler's propaganda Minister, Joseph Goebbels, blasted his film *The Burning Secret* (*Brennendes Geheimnis*). Goebbels, a high-ranking official of a genocidal regime, objected to the movie's plot point of adultery. Siodmak was Jewish. When Hitler threatened France, Siodmak left for California in 1939. He gave false information to obtain a visa. To this day, you will read Siodmak was born in Memphis, Tennessee.

After working as an assistant director, Siodmak teamed up as a director with cinematographer John Seitz for the crime comedy Fly-*By- Night*. Seitz shot a string of great noirs including *This Gun for Hire* 1942, *Five Graves to Cairo* 1943, *Double Indemnity* 1944, The *Lost Weekend* 1945, *The Big Clock* 1948 (a noir thriller with a wonderful comic performance by Elsa Lanchester), *and Sunset Boulevard* 1950.

 The *Fly-By-Night* art director was German Hans Dreier (*Five Graves to Cairo* 1943, *Double Indemnity* 1944, The *Lost Weekend* 1945, *and Sunset Boulevard* 1950).

Fly-By- Night has snatches of witty dialogue and humorous scenes when characters think Nancy Kelly is flirting with them when she is trying to wink in the direction of murder suspect Richard Carlson. The writer was Jay Dratler, *Laura* 1944, *The Dark Corner* 1946, and *Call Northside 777* 1948. It was remarkable that such emerging noir talents gathered for this modest B-movie.

Towards the end of *Fly-By-Night*, an attractive bit of business involving a weapon provides well-shot, simple but effective special effects.

The verdict: *Fly-By-Night* ★ ★ ★

Siodmak's next films for Universal were B-horrors *Son of Dracula* 1943, and the cult favorite *Cobra Woman* 1944, starring Dominican actor Maria Montez.

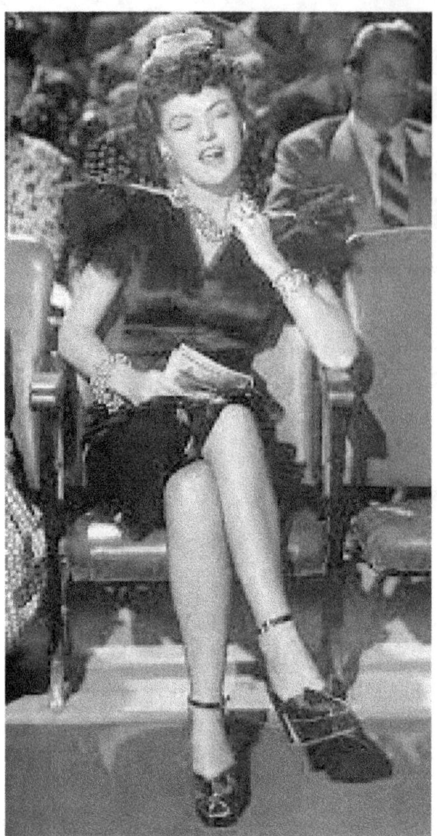

I am yet to solve the mystery of what is hanging to our right of Elisha. People suggested it reflected a dancer in a mirror. But this scene is not set in a nightclub or concert hall. It is a concrete bunker where manic jazz musicians, fuelled by alcohol, jam chaotically. Raines feeds Cook drinks, and he simulates a sex act with his kit. Spectacular filmmaking. I think the wall hanging is a dead animal, reflecting the wildness of the jazzmen. It is a shame that no one has asked Siodmak for an explanation. If anyone can definitively solve this mystery, I will be grateful.

The verdict: *Phantom Lady* ★★★⯪☆

Chapter 8: Dark ventures

Cook's two 1944 films after *Phantom Lady* were both noirs, *Dark Mountain* and *Dark Waters*. A quality chasm separated the humdrum Mountain from the sparkling Waters.

Irony: Elisha makes the poster for the dull movie but not for the good one.

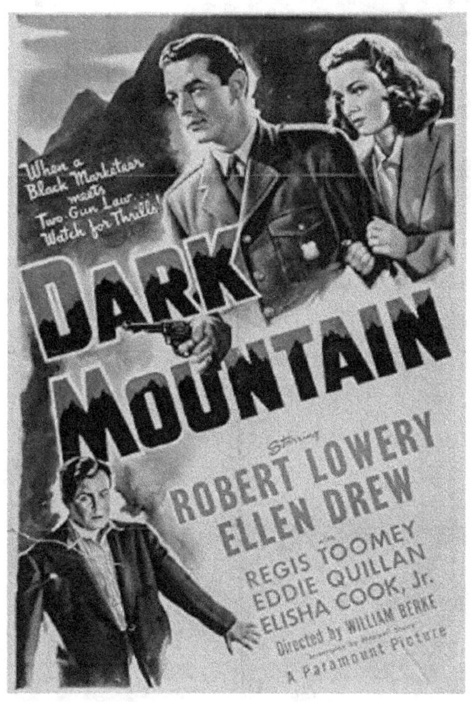

Dark Mountain and *Dangerous Passage* were the first films of B-specialist Pine-Thomas Productions attached to Paramount Studios. Pine-Thomas had made a string of low-budget adventure movies that had returned multiples on modest investments. By the late 1940s, Pine-Thomas changed its strategy to produce films with bigger budgets such as Joseph Losey's *The Lawless* 1950.

Dark Mountain director William Berke specialized in B-Westerns and noirs during his lengthy career. With low budgets, shooting times of less than two weeks, and casts of little-knowns, he unfortunately did not make one memorable noir between 1944 (*Dangerous Passage* was his first) and his death on the set of the sci-fi-B *The Lost Missile* 1958.

Besides Cook, *Dark Mountain* had good actors, Regis Toomey, and Ellen Drew, as well as nefarious deeds and Elisha duplicity, but the whole thing was contrived and unbelievable rather than suspenseful. An amateur reviewer wrote of this film, "Anything with Elisha Cook, Jr. - count me in!" As big a fan of Elisha as I am, I cannot be that generous of spirit. I plagiarize Samuel Goldwyn to say, include me out.

The Verdict: *Dark Mountain* 

We are introduced early in *Dark Waters* to the eccentric Fay Bainter, pictured right of Franchot Tone and Merle Oberon, and it looks like the movie is morphing into a comedy. As they say in movie cliché, nothing could be further from the truth. Bainter won best support for the Bette Davis period melodrama *Jezebel* 1938. It is no surprise to see perennial villain and all-round fine actor Thomas Mitchell is not what he seems.

The Player

Dark deeds: Mitchell and Cook take in some night air in *Dark Waters*.

As a young man, Thomas Mitchell combined theatrical acting and the family profession of journalism. In 1927, aged 35, Mitchell decided to make acting his career. He joined the Lambs Club, an arts patronage group named after brother-and-sister writers Charles and Mary Lamb (*Tales from Shakespeare* 1807). The club had a noirish tinge as Mary had knifed her mother to death, bringing slaughter to the Lambs.

Mitchell's 13th film role was lucky when he won the Oscar for best support playing an alcoholic doctor in the John Ford Western *Stagecoach* 1939.

Dr. Josiah Boone: Three weeks ago I took a bullet out of a man who was shot by a gentleman. The bullet was in his back.

Mitchell's first noir was *Angels Over Broadway* 1940, best remembered for its teaming of Douglas Fairbanks Jr. and Rita Hayworth in the leads. Mitchell was good as a dispirited playwright in a noir set in the New York theater district, but too theatrical for its own good. Some describe Angels as a proto-noir. I accept it as a noir, but not the first. Angels debuted in cinemas in October. *Stranger on the First Floor* appeared in August.

His other noirs before *Dark Waters* were *Flight from Destiny* 1941, *Out of the Fog* 1941, and *Moontide* 1942.   Later noirs included *The Dark Mirror* 1946, *Alias Nick Beal* 1949, *Journey into Light* 1951 and *While the City Sleeps* 1956. In that last noir, Mitchell returned to his career roots, playing the managing editor of a newspaper.

The Player

During her career in Hollywood, beautiful Merle Oberon hid her ethnicity as the daughter of a Eurasian mother. She said she was born in my country of Australia to white parents, and her birth records were destroyed in a fire. As her real heritage was discovered only after her death, we do not know whether it was fear of racial prejudice or her own embarrassment that led to her chronic deception. Rumors of sexual scandals in the family could have accounted for such embarrassment.

Growing up poor in India, Oberon moved as a teen to France and England. Her first major role was as Anne Boleyn in The Private Life of Henry VIII 1933. In America, she was nominated for the best actor Academy Award for the drama *The Dark Angel* 1935. Her first noir was *The Lodger* 1944. Other noirs were *Temptation* 1946 and *The Price of Fear* 1956. That last film started and ended well, with sludge in between.

The Player

Dark Waters support Rex Ingram was in the war noir *Sahara 1943* and *Moonrise* 1948.

In an indictment of the industry, it was in 1962 that a Black actor first received a contract for a television soap opera.

The series was *The Brighter Day* which began in 1954. Rex Ingram served two weeks of his contract before the show was cancelled.

The Director

Andre de Toth was an Hungaian/ American director who built a reputation for noirs of low to moderate budgets.

He created a memorable ending for *Dark Waters* with exuberant performances from Cook and Mitchell.

De Toth's other noirs included *The Other Love* 1947, *Pitfall* 1948, *Crime Wave* 1954, and *Hidden Fear* 1957.

One of his seven wives was noir star Veronica Lake of the iconic hairstyle. The couple was married between 1944 and 1952. Though both were noted for their noirs, they did not make one together. The two films they did together were the Western *Ramrod* 1946 and the drama *Slattery's Hurricane* 1949. The couple is pictured above.

Ladd of the Lake:

The three noirs Lake made with Alan Ladd were all good. They were *This Gun for Hire* 1942, director Frank Tuttle; *The Glass Key* 1942, director Stuart Heisler; and *The Blue Dahlia* 1946, director George Marshall.

Veronica Lake lived a troubled life with maternal reports of mental illness as a child, a lack of confidence and early success spurring altercations with co-stars. She died, aged 50, of alcohol-related medical conditions.

Trivia (but not for them)

Noir directors had an eye for the great shot. One-eyed directors included Andre de Toth, Raoul Walsh (*High Sierra* 1941, Fritz Lang (proto-noir *Fury* 1936 and John Ford (proto-noir *The Informer* 1935). Lang was noted for crime films and Ford for Westerns, but I recall their proto-noirs as a reminder that film noir began before 1940.

The scriptwriter/ producer

Joan Harrison was educated at Oxford and the Sorbonne, so what was this cultured Englishwoman doing in Hollywood writing a script for *Dark Waters* and producing *Phantom Lady?* The answer is Alfred Hitchcock.

In 1933, a friend alerted 26-year-old Harrison to an ad in the *Daily Telegraph*.

Wanted: Young Lady. Highest educational qualifications, must be able to speak, read, and write French and German fluently, by producer of films.

The ad did not specify, must be blonde, but the sinister sexual sublimation of practicing Catholic Alfred Hitchcock required that condition. Blonde Harrison got the job.
 – Lane, C. *Phantom Lady: Hollywood Producer Joan Harrison, the Forgotten Woman Behind Hitchcock,* page 1, *Chicago Review Press*. Kindle.

Harrison and Hitchcock went to Hollywood. After four years of hits such as *Rebecca* 1940, *Foreign Correspondent* 1940, *Suspicion* 1941, and *Shadow of a Doubt* 1943, Harrison struck out on her own, producing *Phantom Lady* and co-writing *Dark Waters*. She was the first female producer attached to a major studio, Universal.

As a producer, Harrison put together *The Strange Affair of Uncle Harry 1945* (Strange from the title on, I like the tale), *Nocturne* 1946 (entertaining but contrived), *Ride the Pink Horse* 1947 (a classic), and *They Won't Believe Me* 1947 (good).

"When Universal Pictures vetoed her preferred ending for the film *The Strange Affair of Uncle Harry*, she broke her contract and walked off the lot for good."
– Lane, C. p. 7.

Film critic/ screenwriter:
James Agee

"The two people most to be thanked for so intelligently casting, specifying, and bringing to life this generally superior movie are the producer, Joan Harrison, and the director, Robert Siodmak. Nobody is to be thanked for the asinine ending."

– Agee J. review of *The Strange Affair of Uncle Harry*, *The Nation*, August 25, 1945, in *Agee on Film, Vol. 1.* 1961, New York Grosset & Dunlap, page 170.

From his comments, Agee knew Siodmak refused to re-shoot the changed ending, shot by by uncredited Roy William Neill (*Black Angel* 1946).

To add insult to Harrison's inury, Universal asked viewers not to disclose their silly ending as if it was some stroke of ingenuity that would awe audiences.

When Universal appointed Harrison to direct *Phantom Lady*, media objectified her rather than praising her skills or her representation of the advancement of women. The New York Times wrote of her "dimples and 24-inch-waistline." Gossip merchant Hedda Hopper dubbed her "Glamour Girl Number One". The *Los Angeles Times* noted, for the record, that Harrison was a a "blonde, blue-eyed babe".

– Lane, C. page 141.

Universal did not extend Harrison's contract beyond *Phantom Lady*, which made the cynics think the deal was a gimmick tied to the woman-centric noir. Independent producer Benedict Bogeaus hired Harrison for *Dark Waters*.

After the success of *Dark Waters*, Universal invited the prodigal daughter back into the studio fold and gave her choice of progect. Harrison chose the succesful and expensive play *The Strange Affair of Uncle Harry*. Dysfunctional siblings George Sanders and Geraldine Fitzgerald are pictured below.

When Universal squibbed it on Uncle Harry's ending, Harrison, director Robert Siodmak and Geraldine Fitzgerald reused to participate in a re-shoot. Fitzgerald's absence made the new ending even sillier. An inauthentic ending can detract from enjoyment of a good noir. I regard Uncle Harry and *The Woman in the Window* 1944 as two of the worst offenders. Harrison walked out on her three-picture contract with Universal. The studio did not sue.

The story goes that Irish actor Geraldine Fitzgerald, left, lost the part of Brigid O'Shaughnessy in *The Maltese Falcon* after a fight with Jack Warner over the quality of her roles.

While John Huston does not mention this in his autobiography, *An Open Book*, Fittzgerald would not have been the only actor in dispute with the Lord of the Warner Brothers fiefdom. While Mary Astor showed excellent range in the Falcon, Fitzgerald would have done an admirable job.

Fitzgerald's first noir teamed her with Thomas Mitchell in *Flight from Destiny* 1941 that had the premise of a man with only months to live pondering whether to kill an evil person.

Fitzgerald's other noirs were *Three Strangers* 1946, and *Nobody Lives Forever* 1946. Fitzgerald spent most of the 1950s working in theater. Her film career revived and included playing female lead in the neo-noir classic *The Pawnbroker* 1964.

Noir specialist studio RKO courted Joan Harrison after her acrimonious departure from Universal. RKO offered Harrison a standard noir mystery with the twist: it centred on the title's musical number, *Nocturne*, composed by Leigh Harline, who enjoyed creating a darker piece than his award-winning compositions for Disney animated musicals. *Nocturne* 1946 was a box-office success.

Harrison's next movie *They Won't Believe Me* 1947 bombed despite it being a good noir with a strong cast of Susan Hayward, Robert Young and newcomer Jane Greer, future Kathie Moffat in *Out of the Past* 1947.

Dictatorial Howard Hughes took over RKO and Joan Harrison left.

Harrison rode her merry-go-round horse from RKO to actor/ director Robert Montgomery's company, Neptune Productions. Montgomery had parted ways with MGM after the ultimately pointless gimmick of the subjective camera for *Lady in the Lake* 1947 which Montgomery starred in and directed.

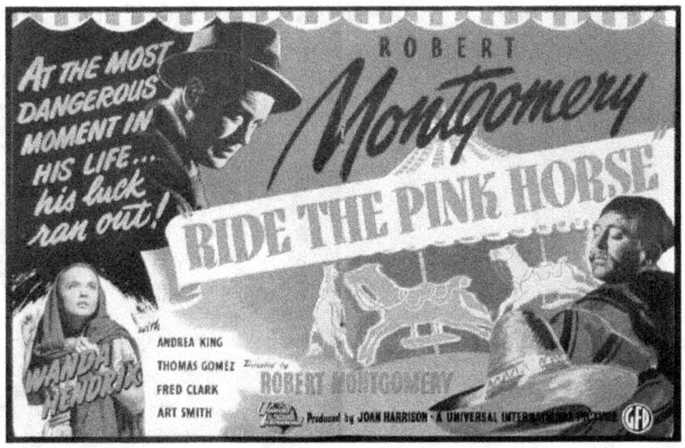

With his new company Montgomery linked with Universal for *Ride the Pink Horse* 1947 and Harrison was back at the ranch of unpleasant memories. I suspect the liberal Harrison had influence over the conservative Montgomery to create an awesome film noir, well regarded by critics at its cimematic debut, but shamefully neglected over the decades since.

Joan Harrison and Montgomery were unable to recapture the magic of the pink horseride. In the 1950s, they went their separate ways into television, a medium through which Harrison and Hitchcock reunited.

The Cinematographer

For cinematographer John J. Mescall, *Dark Waters* was his last film and only noir. He was 45 years old, so it was more a case of the movies leaving him than he leaving the movies. Mescall was an alcoholic who found it more congenial to be a consultant on sophisticated photography rather than endure the rigors of completing a film. Despite his sole contribution to noir, Mescall was an important contributor to its predecessor, the horror movie.

Mescall's first horror was the silent *The Leopard Lady* 1928. The movie is noted for make-up artist Charles Gemora starting a lucrative sideline playing apes, opposite Lon Chaney, *The Unholy Three* 1930; Bela Lugosi, *Murders in the Rue Morgue* 1932, Laurel and Hardy, *The Chimp* 1932; The Marx Brothers, *At the Circus* 1939; Bob Hope and Bing Crosby, *Road to Zanzibar* 1941; Abbott and Costello, *Africa Screams 1949*; and Robert Mitchum, *White Witch Doctor* 1953.

Mescall talkie horrors were *The Black Cat* 1934, and *Bride of Frankenstein* 1935. Mescall was well chummy with Frankenstein (Boris Karloff).

But romance couldn't ensue. The Monster was betrothed to another (Elsa Lanchester).

Lanchester shone in the gothic noir comedy *Ladies in Retirement* 1941 as a weird sister to sensible Ida Lupino, and the equally weird sister Edith Barrett.

Lupino, the youngest of the three played the oldest. She was 23, Barrett was 34, and Lanchester, 39. The film is great fun.

Elisha Cook Jr. had a significant role in *Dark Waters,* so he should have been nicer to Wardrobe, and they might have given him more than one jacket. Thomas Mitchell prances about in a white suit because he is on a sugar plantation and he wants to convince everyone he is a good guy.

Franchot Tone is a good guy in this one, and he wears grey suits to show he is the solid reliable sort that Merle should fall for.

The verdict: *Dark Waters* ★★★⯨☆

Chapter 9: Alibis don't stack up

Cook was in three noirs released in 1946. The first two were bombs: *Blonde Alibi* and *The Falcon's Alibi*. The third was *The Big Sleep*. It was a case or two cases of going from the ridiculous to the sublime.

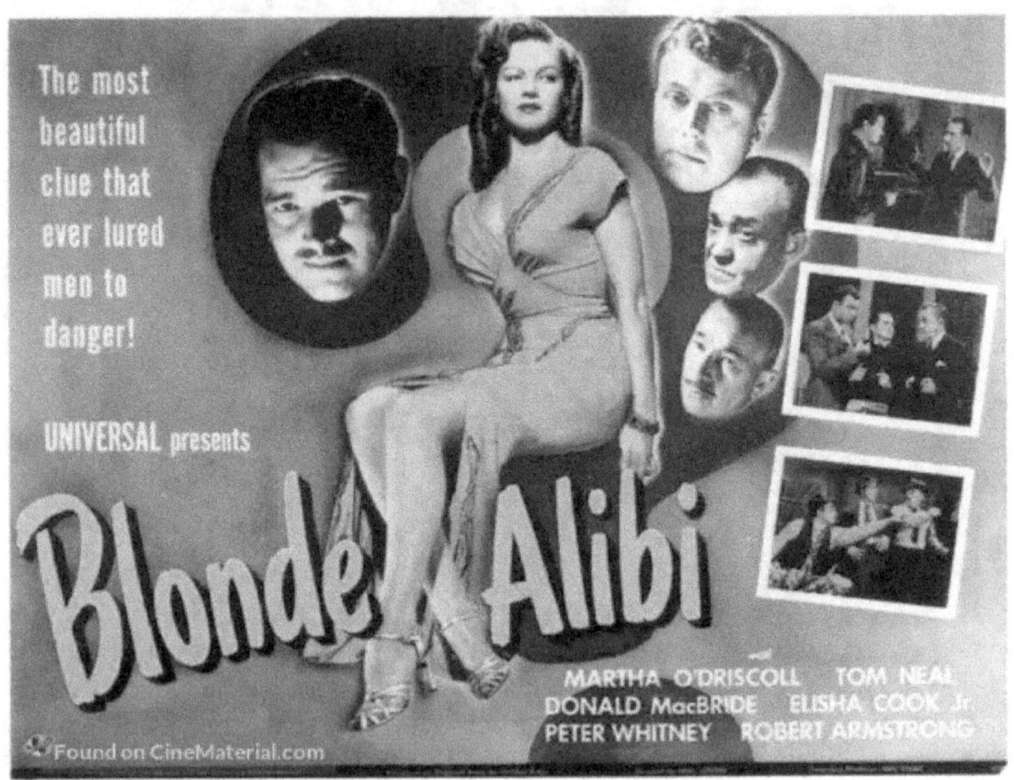

There is a pattern emerging in Elisha's crime movies, or an M.O., as we like to say in the pulps or maybe the slicks. Okay, I will explain before I continue my philosophical thesis. Pulps were the inexpensive crime magazines of the 1930s and 1940s. Slicks were the glossy magazines which paid crime writers more. The irony was that stories in the slicks were more formulaic, as they had to adhere to editorial policies. Pulp writers were allowed to be inventive. M.O. referred to *modus operandi*, a presumption that criminals, like stories in the slicks, followed a pattern of operation.

Where was I? Oh yes, the Cook crime movie M.O. If Elisha made the poster, it would likely be an inferior product, *Blonde Alibi* is a case in point. A corpse lies in the street after a hit and run. A paramedic tells a cop, "Dead on arrival", a phrase that refers to arrival at a hospital. The cop calls a paramedic, "Doc". Such sloppy attention to detail derails a B-noir.

Cook plays a cabbie who thinks he has killed the man who was shot before he stumbled into the front of the cab. Elisha is another terrified loser. We like it. As David Thomson wrote, "Put him in a bad picture, and he made it watchable for 10 minutes."

– Thomson D. page 174.

Cook has a good scene in which a police detective hails his cab to take him to police headquarters. Cook demands his fare. Cook thinks he has been lumbered for the hit and run, but it is over another matter of which Elisha is innocent. Elisha not only demands his fare, but he also brazenly says to the cop, "What, no tip?" On his way out, a witness recognizes Cook about the hit-and-run. "I knew things were going too good to last," Cook says. We've seen your other pictures, Elisha, we're hearing you.

The film's ambience lurches carelessly from thrills to comedy, and neither mode is of high quality. Male lead Tom Neal (*Detour* 1945) appears at 20 minutes of the 62-minute cheapie to lift the acting.

Neal was an ex-boxer who should have committed to the box office rather than public brawling. After a vicious assault on Franchot Tone, his career plummeted. If you wish, you can read more about the sordid life of Tom Neal, whom *Detour* co-star Ann Savage astutely described as emotionally "a child". As it turned out, a dangerous child.

Female lead Martha O'Driscoll was a blonde, but that did not explain the title in a film that had more plot holes than a graveyard. O'Driscoll gave acting away in 1947. In 1984, she co-founded Appleton Museum of Art in Florida.

NY's MoMA shows quality film noir. If Appleton's did the same, *Blonde Alibi* would not be on any bill. Inspecting their website, I could see no noirs, but in May 2025, the museum screened a free double bill of the famed Japanese monster movies *Godzilla* 1954, and *The Return of Godzilla* 1984 (no, not about the re-election of Ronald Reagan).

Brothers: Left to right are Tom Conway, George Sanders, Ray and Leo McCarey.

The Falcon's Alibi could have the subtitle *My Famous Brother*. George Sanders handed up his role as the Falcon to his older brother, Tom Conway. They were born less than two years apart, looked remarkably similar, and had similar English upper-class accents. Well, they sounded upper-class to me, but I am no Professor Henry Higgins. The brothers were both born in Russia and lived there until Tom was 13 when they relocated to England.

Like Tom Conway, *The Falcon's Alibi* director Ray McCarey was born in 1904. He was the younger brother of Leo McCarey by six years. Ray directed mainly comedies after training at the Hal Roach studios. Leo McCarey also worked in comedies, but with bigger budgets and more success: *Duck Soup* 1933, *The Awful Truth* 1937, *Once Upon a Honeymoon* 1942, *Going My Way* 1944, and *The Bells of St. Mary's* 1945. He also directed the popular romance *An Affair to Remember* 1957.

One fun part of *The Falcon's Alibi* was Elisha Cook Jr.'s impersonation of a disc jockey, with fast patter. He spun a record by the (Nat) King Cole Trio.

Other highlights were Jane Greer, the future femme fatale Kathie Moffat of *Out of the Past* 1947, singing and performing two songs. Greer could both sing and interpret songs well. Fellow femme fatale Lizabeth Scott could do neither, yet producers kept casting her in roles of a lounge singer.

Nonsense that sorta worked was one of the horses in a race being called Ginger Rogers.

The acting limitations of many in the cast were obvious, so they left the dramatic parts of the comedy-mystery-noir-thriller to the married couple, played by Cook and Greer.

Elisha, you just gotta stop batting out of your league. You should know by now, it is going to end in tears. And it does.

Unfortunately, a lame script with only a few unpolished gems of wit let the actors down.

The plot was stolen from Raymond Chandler's 1942 novel *The High Window*. As the wit said, the only "ism" in classic Hollywood was plagiarism.

Cook's role in *The Big Sleep* 1946 is as impressive a turn as that of Wilmer Cook in *The Maltese Falcon*. Better. I say that because it is more human. Wilmer's fake tough-guy degenerate murderer was fabulous. Harry Jones in *The Big Sleep* is an insecure little guy who falls in love with wrong'un Agnes (Sonia Darrin) looking for a sap after a pornography racket fell apart. Agnes is Lowzier in the movie, Lozelle in the novel.

A conversation between Agnes and Marlowe sums up the relationship between Harry and her: For some weird reason Darrin was uncredited, and her character's family name was changed from that in the novel. In both novel and movie, Agnes is key to plot development.

Agnes: Wish me luck. I got a raw deal.
Marlowe: Hey, your kind always does.

Darrin's was one of many fine turns of bit players, a tribute to Howard Hawks, director of *The Big Sleep*.

Harry Jones is aware of his slight physical build that affords him no safety in a world of criminals. In an exchange with Bogart, he rationalises keeping a low profile.
Marlowe: Swell. Did you want to see those guys jump me?
Harry: I didn't care one way or the other.
Marlowe: You could've yelled for help.
Harry: If a guy's playing a hand, I let him play it. I'm no kibitzer.

Jones loses his dispassion when he falls in love with Agnes and he develops inner strength that defies his outward fear.
Lash Canino (Bob Steele): You want me to count three or something like in the movies?

Everything is near perfect in *The Big Sleep* from the novel's title, a euphemism for murder, to the sharp dialogue, faithful to the novel. It was a shame the film omitted this strangely attractive line:
Vivian Rutledge: "I ought to throw a Buick at you."

They kept:
Marlowe: "(My manners) are pretty bad. I grieve over them long winter evenings."

Cook is not menacing or boastful, but a small honest guy trying to settle down with Agnes in a rough, uncaring world. He negotiates with Marlowe in good faith to sell a deadly secret. This is a more subdued approach to a role from Cook but his characteristic ability to mold his face to tell the story behind his words prevails. The camera and the protagonist Marlowe watch on in admiration. Harry dispassionately recounts his association with criminals, and Marlowe sarcastically agrees with him:

Harry: I've been around too. Used to run a little liquor. Rode the scout car with a Tommy gun in my lap. Tough racket.

Marlowe: Terrible!

Harry is not expressing the bravura of a Wilmer Cook but the tiredness of a man who wants to escape from a blood-stained world.

Untrue:

An enduring myth about the film being confusing, especially about the Sternwood chauffeur is just not true.

The myth began when author Chandler was reported to have been asked who killed the chauffeur and confessed to not knowing what happened to the Sternwood's driver.

Watch this scene and it will tell you who killed Owen Taylor, the chauffeur.

Deadly Eddie: John Ridgely plays sinister Eddie Mars and Martha Vickers is Carmen Sternwood. Below Bogie and Bacall await Mars for the climax.

Who killed Sean Regan is explained in the two scenes, above, the second before the action climax. Admittedly Bogart speaks fast throughout much of the film that I have watched many times. I can forgive confused contemporary critics who had to write reviews after one screening. But to pan Bacall's acting as *New York Times* critic Bosley Crowther did was grossly unfair. Bacall comes across as confident and witty, matching Bogart's wisecracks. That must have been quite an effort for the twenty year old film tyro.

Couples: Dorothy Malone & Humphrey Bogart

Elisha Cook Jr. and Bob

My two favorite scenes are studies in contrast. Bookshop manager Malone and Bogart flirt over rare books, while rain teems down outside. Funny, clever, and sensual, the scene is a wonder to behold as well as moving the plot along.

Bob Steele trying to terrify the courageous Elisha Cook Jr. see the bit players at their peak, exhibiting menace and resilience, repectively.

I calculated Cook's total screen time in *The Big Sleep* at under seven minutes which included when we only heard his voice or he was not able to talk. But he stamped those seven minutes with a support performance that will be remembered as long as movie lovers reach back in the past to be awed by the actor who failed to make the film posters.

Lash Canino: What's funny?
Harry Jones: Nothing's funny.

Joy Barlow, as a cab driver, rendered another good bit part. It was a nod to wartime employment where women took traditional male jobs to replace the men serving overseas. Marlowe was not the most handsome shamus in the business – that would be Mike Hammer in *Kiss Me Deadly* 1955. But young women lined up or drove up to flirt with Marlowe.

Barlow: If you can use me again sometime, call this number.
Bogie: Day and night?
Barlow: Uh, night's better. I work during the day.

Two Bills: Bill Hunter the big guy, at left, shared his name with the acclaimed Australian actor, right.

The U.S. Hunter was uncredited in *Destination Tokyo* 1943, as was Joy Barlow who played the girlfriend of Wolf (John Garfield).

Joy Barlow played in nineteen movies, released between 1941 and 1952. She was uncredited in eighteen of them. Well, to be fair, one in 1944 was a short, promoting Bob Wills and His Texas Playboys country swing band, so let's say seventeen features, uncredited. The other noir classic Barlow was in was *To Have and Have Not*, 1944, also with Bogart and Bacall and directed by Howard Hawks.

Joy Barlow's credited role was in Republic Pictures *The Trespasser* 1947. The B-studio had the habit of listing many of its actors. The bit players might become stars one day and the veterans deserved recognition for endurance. Her family name was listed as Barlowe, a transcription error. With cinematography by noir genius John Alton and patches of witty dialogue, it is not a bad movie, but it is strangely constructed. It is twenty minutes before we get to the meat of the crime, and 26 minutes of a 69-minute film before the lead Dale Evans appears.

For Evans, it was a departure from her burgeoning romantic and business partnership with the horse-opera singing cowboy Roy Rogers. That partnership was to last decades through films, television, radio, and musical recordings. Evans, after her late arrival, had minimal screen time, dominated by second female lead Janet Martin whose birthdate is uncertain, but it was likely she was a teenager when the film was made.

What happened to Janet Martin is equally uncertain. But a record exists of how Ms Martin started in the business.

"Seven-year contracts have been given Twinkle Watts and Valya Terry, eight and 14 years old, respectively, by Republic with Miss Terry slated to appear in a musical titled *Melody in June.*"

Motion Picture Herald August 14, 1943, page 44.

Valya Terry, the daughter of a Russian opera singer, became Janet Martin. I know, I know, you want to know what became of Miss Twinkle Watts. Twinkle, little star, did not emulate Shirley Temple, but she did play in eleven movies until 1946. Janet Martin lasted two years longer until 1948, during which she had appeared as a lead female in four films. Then she disappeared, vanished, gone without a trace.

Twinkle and Janet signed seven-year contracts in 1943 and were gone by 1946 and 1948. Even in dodgy film accounting, that was not seven years. Republic continued to make movies until 1958.

Have we got a biopic here! Imagine it: Joy Barlow, Janet Martin, and Miss Twinkle at Republic. The title picks itself. *Falling Stars*. Margot Robbie dyes her hair brunette to play Joy Barlow. Robbie will become a noir star like Joan Bennett. Bye bye, Barbie.

The theme is why they did not make it. Why couldn't Joy progress to better roles? Why didn't Janet capitalize on her promising start at the B-studio? She had talent, so what stopped her? And Miss Twinkle, why was she only a child star for a few short years?

Male Supremacy:

Golden palomino stallion Trigger received higher billing than Dale Evans and Janet Martin in the Western *Bells of Rosarita* 1945.

Trigger was billed above Dale Evans in every Republic picture starring the horse, Roy Rogers, and Evans.

This was unfair. The horse was a good actor, but he could not sing. Trigger could dance a bit, but he was a third short of a triple threat.

Was it because Trigger was a blond, and Evans a brunette?

Page 16: Bacall, Lauren *By Myself* Ballantine Books NY 1980.

The Player

Nineteen-year-old Lauren Bacall made her film debut in *To Have and Have Not* 1944. The chemistry between Bogart and Bacall lit up the big screen as it reflected their romance off-screen. Always nervous before her limited school and stage performances, Betty Perske was overwhelmed at her surprise opportunity to be top billed with Bogie of the hits, *The Maltese Falcon* and *Casablanca*.

"Making a fool of yourself is something all actors have to risk doing. That's part of our business" – Bacall L. 1980 page 30.

Lauren Bacall, formerly Betty Perske, was an introvert but one driven by a compulsion to become a star of stage and screen like her idols Bette Davis and Katharine Hepburn. That amusing scene in which she has an itch above her knee in *The Big Sleep* seemed a reflection of her personality. Bogart tells her to scratch if she needs to and she hurriedly does before replacing her skirt over her knee.

Reinvented Bacal added an extra l to her revised family name for clarity of pronunciation. She was working as a theater usher before *To Have and Have Not*. She was ushering for a play starring comedian/singer/dancer Danny Kaye. Bacall courageously knocked on Kaye's door after a show.

"He asked a few polite questions about my non-existent career and gave me his autograph, for which I thanked him profusely, and left." – Bacall L. 1980 page 45.

The Hollywood folklore that director Howard Hawks' wife "Slim" Keith discovered model Bacall via a magazine photo ignores that the young woman had paid her dues before her first film role. She had spent a year in theater training, and another year pounding the harsh pavements of the New York theater district. Bacall's first professional role was in a play, *Franklin Street*, destined for Broadway. It was by the hit-making team of producer Max Gordon and director George S. Kaufman, (*The Bandwagon*, *My Sister Eileen*). *Franklin Street* never saw Broadway, closing after its Washington run which attracted tepid reviews. Bacall was devastated. Her fortunes did change through her modelling assignments that included a cover of *Harper's Bazaar*.

Photographer: Louise Dahl-Wolfe

David O. Selznick and Howard Hughes sent inquiries to *Harper's Bazaar* after the magazine informed readers that Bacall was an actor. Columbia made a restrictive offer she could and did refuse. Howard Hawks' office called. That was it.

Bacall would stay in Los Angeles for six weeks. Hawks would assess and evaluate her. The pay would be $50 a week. At eighteen, a confirmed New Yorker, hitches her wagon west. Hawks signed her for seven years at escalating salary.

"Either consciously or unconsciously, (Hawks) wanted to be Svengali, and he was to me at the beginning." – Bacall L. 1980 page 110.

Hawkish: Bogart, Bacall and Hawks on the set of *To Have and Have Not* 1944. Being photographed during their break was obviously not their cup of tea.

The first scene Bacall tested for a part in *To Have and Have Not* was the "whistle" scene that serendipitously provided one of the grand quotes from film noir: "You know how to whistle, don'tcha, Steve? You just put your lips together and (pause) blow." The pause before blow nailed it. Steve was not the name of Bogart's character. Steve was Howard Hawks' nickname, and the scene was emblematic of the director's uncanny ability to include innuendo-infused humor into noirs. It could also have been a sign of a control freak, the blessed curse of many a cinematic auteur.

Bacall did not say that Hawks hit on her, but she recounted how Bogart said Hawks was jealous about their affair. The director had threatened to derail Bacall's career. She did say Hawks expressed antisemitism, without knowing Bacall was Jewish. Bacall seems to imply that Hawks had prompted a crew member to suggest she have sex with the director. Because he was such a good filmmaker, critics rarely wrote about the murkier aspects of his character.

Hawks' sublime ability to coach tyro performers was exemplified in the scenes between Bacall and jazz pianist Hoagy Carmichael, both making their debuts in *To Have and Have Not*.

Bacall shot *The Big Sleep* after *To Have and Have Not* but it was shelved for reshoots. Her movie after *The Big Sleep* was *Confidential Agent* 1945, released before *The Big Sleep*. *Confidential Agent* cast and crew promised a good movie. Charles Boyer, pictured with Bacall, was male lead and Peter Lorre supported. Noir genius James Wong Howe was the cinematographer.

Bacall's performance was inexplicably poor. Her character disappeared for large sections of the film. That suggested even poorer footage remained on the cutting-room floor, though much of what survived the final edit was unimpressive.

Bacall and critics commented that she was miscast as a spoilt heir. Such a part was not far removed ftom the role she played in *The Big Sleep*. Despite Bacall's lackluster turn, *Confidential Agent* is a fair to good spy thriller with unusual prottagonists of Spanish Civil War Republican agents. Bacall was probably put off playing a Brit so early in her career. Happily, married to Bogart, she was partially immune to criticism, but the reviews stung. "I wonder if critics realize how destructive they are."
– Bacall L. 1980, page 196.

Fortunately, *The Big Sleep* followed *Confidential Agent*.

another. One day Bogie came on the set and said to Howard, "Who pushed Taylor off the pier?" Everything stopped. Howard, no one, had the answer. Taylor was the mystery chauffeur in the film. His disappearance was what brought Marlowe (Bogie) on the case originally. Howard sent a cable to Raymond Chandler asking him. *He* didn't know. *The Big Sleep* was a whodunit's whodunit. Intricate, intriguing, mys-

Page 159: *Lauren Bacall By Myself* Ballantine Books NY 1980.

Bacall buys into the mythology about the murder of Owen Taylor. She makes an incorrect statement about the chauffeur's disappearance bringing Bogie onto the case. General Sternwood hires Marlowe to fix the blackmail of Sternwood's younger daughter, Carmen (Martha Vickers). The older daughter Vivian (Bacall) suggests her father's ulterior motive was to find out what happened to Sean Regan, the General's colorful assistant. Vivian made no mention of the chauffeur whose murder Marlowe solved later.

The Big Sleep was the only movie Bacall and Elisha Cook Jr. made together. They shared no screen time. Bogart and Bacall made two more films together, *Dark Passage* 1947 and *Key Largo* 1948.

Both are classic noirs. Bogart and Cook only made the two films together.

Alain Silver recognizes the centrality of the interaction of Marlowe and Jones to the theme of trust lost and tarnished trust regained.

"Marlowe's hard guy pose is a thin veneer easily pierced by his admiration for the loyal heroism of a "little man" like Harry Jones."

. . . *The Big Sleep* becomes a series of character encounters in which the drama of trust tendered, trust betrayed, and trust restored is played out. . . . Marlowe needs at least one person to anchor his own shaken code of beliefs. He has one for a brief interlude in Harry Jones and his fidelity to the worthless Agnes."

Silver A, Ward E, Macek C, Porfirio R, and Ursini J. *Film noir: an encyclopedic reference to the American style, Overlook Press*, NY 1992, page 34.

Chapter 11: Sean Penn's Dad

After the high of an acclaimed character role in *The Big Sleep*, Elisha Cook Jr. came down to earth with a noir cheapie, *Fall Guy*. It is a good movie with creative flair replacing dollars as expenditure to produce a satisfying result. The protagonist was Leo Penn, father of actors Sean, and the late Chris (1965-2006), and musician Michael.

It was a case of keeping it the family for one neo-noir. Christopher Walken plays Sean Penn's criminal father in *At Close Range* 1986. Also in the cast were Sean's brother Chris and their real-life mother Eileen Ryan (pictured top with Chris). In one of those inexplicable misfortunes, the movie crashed at the box office. Mind you, Walken efficiently played one of the slimiest characters seen on the big screen. That might have had something to do with it. The film has a high critical rating on *Rotten Tomatoes*.

Fall Guy was Leo Penn's second film, and, despite his distinguished war service, he was blacklisted for a decade after his fourth. Penn had refused to co-operate with the notorious House Un-American Activities Committee. Penn went to the less heavily policed television as an actor, but his blacklisting followed him to the small screen. He moved on to television directing, a job in which he could keep a lower profile.

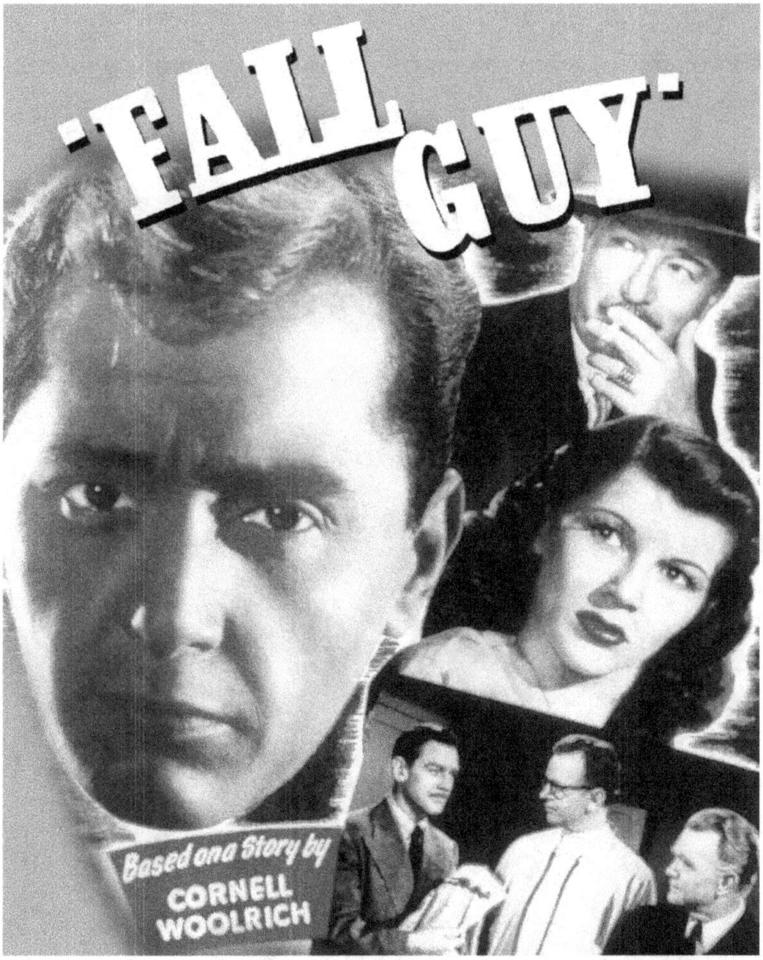

Penn and Cook are guests at a party where a woman is killed, and Penn is shot up with drugs and framed.

Shady elevator operator Cook wants nothing to do with aiding Penn. But Cook, under physical pressure, relents. You know the perennial loser's good deed will not go unpunished.

Chapter 12: Another noir classic

Born To Kill 1947 troubled critics and viewers on its release. *New York Times* critic Bosley Crowther could be extreme in his denunciation of a film he did not like.

"This crime-flaunting melodrama from the left hand of RKO is not only morally disgusting but is an offense to a normal intellect. . . precisely because it is designed to pander to the lower levels of taste that it is reprehensible."

Crowther B. *New York Times*, May 1, 1947, *The Screen* supplement.

Do you think Director Robert Wise made the morally uplifting *The Sound of Music* 1965 as atonement for *Born to Kill*? "Left hand of RKO"? Was RKO a Hollywood god? Doubt it.

While it contains repulsive scenes, *Born to Kill* is a particularly good film with excellent directing, clever plotting, and fine acting from Claire Trevor, Lawrence Tierney, Esther Howard, Walter Slezak, and Elisha Cook Jr. We know it is a good movie as Cook's name fails to appear on the poster. Cook and Howard fail to get nods in publicity, but the film is a five-hand ensemble effort. Each partner receives adequate screen time.

Tierney, a violent sociopath in real life, plays a psychopath in a co-dependent relationship with the equally murderous Cook. I did not detect any hints of a sexual relationship. But they cannot live without each other and victims die because of it.

Elisha Cook Jr. said all the main characters in the favorite movie he was a partner in, *The Maltese Falcon,* were seriously flawed.
"There wasn't one decent person in the whole film," he said.
– Folkart B.A. *Los Angeles Times* obituary, May 20, 1995.

While the truth of Cook's assessment made the Falcon great, its characters were saints compared to the disturbed lot disgracing the screen in *Born to Kill.*

It is not surprising that censors culled *Born to Kill.* What is surprising is that it was not more heavily restricted. Hays Office chief censor Joseph I. Breen wrote internally that it "ought not to be made because it is a story of gross lust and shocking brutality and ruthlessness."

But it was made and included such shocks you wonder what the expunged scenes were.

Cook's last scene in the movie with Howard and Tierney on wind-swept sand dunes is as hauntingly beautiful as it is harrowing. The acting, directing, and camera work by veteran Robert De Grasse combine to create a slice of cinematic beautiful ugliness. The dunes were on El Segundo Beach in southern California. It is four hundred miles from San Franciso to El Segundo, near LA, so the cab fare of Mrs. Kraft (Esther Howard) must have been a doozy. The intersection of Clay and Taylor streets was and is real, but I doubt the El Segundo tourism bureau was happy with the free advert.

The Shooter

Movie partners: Cinematographer Robert De Grasse and actor Claire Trevor worked on *Crack-Up* 1946 before *Born To Kill*.

Robert De Grasse was one of Hollywood's youngest cinematographers, shooting *Desperate Trails* 1921 when he was twenty-one. The director John Ford was 26 years old.

The film is lost but publicity remains including filmmakers exploiting the baby actor Harry Carey Jr.

By the time of *Crack-Up* and *Born to Kill*, De Grasse had shot more than sixty-five films including Katharine Hepburn's feminist role in *A Woman Rebels* 1936 with Van Heflin in his first film. Unfortunately, it was a heavy loser for RKO.

Ironically, Hepburn turned down the lead in another RKO woman-centric film and Ginger Rogers played *Kitty Foyle* 1940, shot by De Grasse. With a screenplay by Dalton Trumbo and Donald Ogden Stewart, the movie was a huge hit.

Famed horror producer Val Lewton and De Grasse put together *The Leopard Man* 1943, panned on release but since upgraded critically. The thing that makes the movie remarkable is the fledgling noir talent it gathered. As well as De Grasse were the director Jacques Tourneur (*Out of the Past* 1947) musical director Roy Webb (*Murder, My Sweet* 1944 and *Out of the Past*) and lead actor Dennis O'Keefe (*T-Men* 1947, *Raw Deal* 1948). Editor Mark Robson went on to direct the noirs *Champion* 1949 and *The Harder They Fall* 1956. The screenplay was based on the 1942 novel *Black Alibi* by prolific contributor to film noir Cornell Woolrich (*Phantom Lady* 1944, *Deadline at Dawn* 1946, *Black Angel* 1946, and *No Man of her Own* 1950).

Be my *Bodyguard*:

After *Born to Kill*, De Grasse's next noir was *Bodyguard* 1948, director Richard Fleischer's first noir and Priscilla Lane's last film. Lane retired to raise a family. Fleischer made B-noirs, *Follow Me Quietly* 1949, *Armored Car Robbery* 1950, and *The Narrow Margin* 1951.

Bodyguard begins with great promise as Tierney quits the police force after suspension for violence. What follows is an entertaining mystery that evades weighty social comment.

Notice that tacky RKO tried to capitalize on Tierney's real-life arrest for assault by showing what looks like him threatening Lane, a total misrepresentation of the plot.

The verdict: *Bodyguard* ★★★½☆

When 1947 rolled around, Claire Trevor, 36 years old, was the veteran of more than forty movies after starting in 1933. Her third film was the crime movie *The Mad Game* 1933 in which she was female lead beside Spencer Tracy. Variety staff reviewed Trevor's performance:

"Trevor impels an exciting interest. About the best portrayal of a newspaper gal which the studios have submitted. Hers is a fine performance." *Variety* Dec 31, 1932.

Variety reviewers knew how to deliver the common touch, the way they praised that acting gal. What a doll! Trevor and Tracy were together again in *Dante's Inferno* 1935.

Hell of a picture: Trevor was with Spencer Tracy for *Dante's Inferno*. Between them above was Scotty Beckett, a child star later stricken by alcohol and dead aged 38. Rita (Cansino) Hayworth, 16, played Dancer.

The 1937 proto-noir *Dead End* brought future noir stars Trevor and Humphrey Bogart together and in the company of 1930s Crime Queen Sylvia Sidney. The director was William Wyler (*The Letter* 1940, *The Little Foxes* 1941, *Detective Story* 1951). Trevor plays a prostitute who was the childhood sweetheart of gangster Bogart, returning home. Trevor was nominated for an Oscar as best support. The cinematographer was Gregg Toland (*Citizen Kane* 1941, *The Little Foxes*). Despite the talent *Dead End* underwhelms me. Production stylized it in pursuit of faux realism, and it is too obviously a morality tale. I did like the support players Marjorie Main and Trevor Jenkins.

Bit players: Main, left, and Jenkins, above.

What J.T. said:

"Of the smaller parts, Claire Trevor's moment as Francey and Marjorie Main's flat-voiced hate as Martin's mother are memorable."
– John T. McManus *New York Times* August 25, 1937, page 25.

People of a venerable age will recall Main as Ma Kettle beside Percy Kilbride (Pa Kettle) in eight hillbilly comedy movies from 1947 to 1956. (Nine movies if you count their introduction as supports in *The Egg and I* 1947). Sick of typecasting limiting other opportunities, Kilbride passed on the final movie. Parker Fennelly replaced him.

Playing a prostitute continued to be beneficial to Trevor's career as she received good notices for *Stagecoach* 1939, for which she received top billing over John Wayne. She repeated her top billing for another Western, *Dark Command* 1940. After that, she rode off from the oaters into the darkening sunset of film noir with *Crossroads* 1942. Trevor played a femme fatale in this successful remake of a French film. It is a strange movie starting off with an implausible courtroom scene followed by an attractive, well acted and photographed nystery that loses steam towards the end when the mystery is solved too soon, followed by much telling instead of showing. Hedy Lamarr proved deft at light comedy but her character of the doting wife lacked oomph.

In that same year of 1942 another release was the noir mystery *Street of Chance* which paired Trevor with Burgess Meredith. The cinematographer was veteran German-born Theodor Sparkuhl who shot the noir *The Glass Key*, 1942, and one of my favourite childhood movies on television, the comedy mystery horror *Murder, He Says* 1945. After you watch this one, family and friends will think you are batty for constantly singing:

Honors Flyzis, Income Beezis
Onches nobis, Inob Keezis.

You are warned.

Noir life is chancy:

In *Street of Chance,* unsettling photography by Sparkuhl reflects the inner turmoil of amnesiac Burgess Meredith, pursued by an ominous Sheldon Leonard for unknown reasons. Sparkuhl's cinematography and Leonard's stern characterization are highlights of the film. And yes, television sitcom *The Big Bang Theory* characters Sheldon Cooper and Leonard Hofstadter were named to honor Sheldon Leonard.

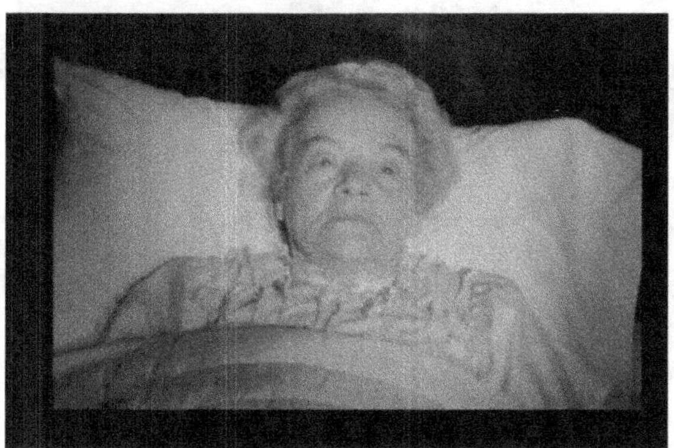

A third of the 74-min *Street of Chance* is over before Trevor makes her entry. The film clicks into a higher gear as she takes command of evading the dogged Leonard. From then on, the movie is hers, though Meredith does clever business in extracting information from a speechless bed-ridden grandma, played by the wonderful Adeline De Walt Reynolds who began her film career aged seventy-eight in *Come Live with Me* 1941. She played her last movie role in *The Ten Commandments* 1956, and she was ninety-eight when she played her last part on television. Vale Adeline.

Street of Chance musical director David Buttolph scored top-quality 1940s' noirs including *Swamp Water* 1941, *This Gun for Hire* 1942, *Moontide* 1942, *The House on 92nd Street* 1945, *Boomerang* (or *Boomerang!*) 1947, *Moss Rose* 1947, and *Kiss of Death* 1947.

In the 1950s, he scored the cult 3-D horror movie *The House of Wax* 1953, as well as the big-monster pioneer *The Beast from 20,000 Fathoms* 1953.

His 1950s noirs impressed less than the 40s films.

French critic Nino Frank in 1946 reviewed four Hollywood films made during World War II to derive a genre he called "film noir". One of the four was *Murder, My Sweet* 1944. The others were *The Maltese Falcon* (1941 the U.S. not yet in the European war), *Laura* 1944, and *Double Indemnity* 1944.

Frank N. *A New Kind of Police Drama: the Criminal Adventure* in *L'Écran Français*, 28 August 1946. (If you think l'écran does not look like the French word for cinema, you are right, it is screen).

Murder, My Sweet explains what Phillip Marlowe was up to before his big sleep. As Marlowe, Dick Powell made the inspired and inspirational transition from crooning to crime. Claire Trevor moved from a 1943 Western relapse to femme fatality.

Anne Shirley played the good gal (thanks *Variety for* "gal"). It was Shirley's last film. She married the film's producer Adrian Scott after she divorced John Payne who followed Powell's example and moved into film noir in the 1950s. Shirley left Scott after he was blacklisted. Or maybe he left her when he headed to Europe for work and she stayed in the U.S.A. They divorced in 1949.

Crime specialist George Raft rarely impressed me with his acting, the exceptions being roles in *Johnny Angel* (1945, with Claire Trevor) and *Whistlestop* (1946, with Ava Gardner, pictured above right). I like the title *Johnny Angel* for this watery noir as it is so inappropriate for the always dour-faced Raft. A better name would have been John Wood, or even Lief Raft. Trevor is again a femme fatale, a former flame of Lief. She is now married to his boss.

Trevor plays a good gal in *Crack-Up* so Hollywood publicity misled potential viewers by posting a caricature of her in a slinky revealing dress.

The reliable plotline of amnesia gets a run, beside an unusual populist critique of modern art. Robert De Grasse lends his cinematographic skill to the mystery and the result is enjoyable.

Anthony Mann's classic *Raw Deal* seized the screens in 1948 with top photography from noir master John Alton. The three leads, Dennis O'Keefe, Marsha Hunt, and Claire Trevor were good, but Trevor was outstanding as the vulnerable woman acting tough.

On her third nomination, Trevor got her just reward of an Oscar for best support in 1948's

Although well regarded by film goers, *Key Largo* rarely attains the position it deserves in lists of best film noirs. In the ensemble cast, Trevor is poignant as the washed-up ex nightclub singer humiliated by gangster Edward G. Robinson. The ability to unsuccessfully hide vulnerability behind a sharp tongue was the special gift Claire Trevor brought to film noir. It made her one of the great female noir leads beside Barbara Stanwyck, Ida Lupino, Joan Bennett, and Gloria Grahame.

The *Key Largo* director was John Huston.

The cinematographer was Karl Freund who, before Hollywood, shot the European classics *The Golem* 1920, *The Last Laugh* 1924, and *Metropolis* 1927. In Hollywood, he photographed the Expressionist horrors *Dracula* 1931 and *Murders in the Rue Morgue* 1932. Before *Key Largo*, Freund shot Katharine Hepburn's only noir *Undercurrent* 1946. The last is a good film, with candid Hepburn, but it is slow in getting down to noir tacks.

The director

Look up "eclectic" in an illustrated dictionary and there is a picture of *Born to Kill* director Robert Wise. The same goes for "classic".

Wise was an editor on *Citizen Kane* for which he received an Academy Award nomination. His directorial debut created the psychological horror classic *The Curse of the Cat People* 1944, with photography by Nicholas Musuraca, and production by Val Lewton. He directed the noir classic *The Set-Up* 1949 starring Robert Ryan and Audrey Totter, with cinematography by Milton R. Krasner. Wise directed the 1951 sci-fi classic *The Day the Earth Stood Still*.

He directed the much-loved musicals *West Side Story* 1961 and *The Sound of Music* 1965.

Wise directed interesting but not brilliant Westerns *Blood in the Moon* 1948, *Two Flags West* 1950, *So Big* 1953, and *Tribute to a Bad Man* 1956.

Wise was 65 years old when he directed *Star Trek The Motion Picture* 1979, based on the TV series. Critically panned, it was a big hit at the box office.

Word to the Wise: Robert Wise is in front of Gort, the robot from *The Day the Earth Stood Still*. Gort is saying to Wise: *Klaatu Barada Nikto*.

Wise replies, I'm gonna use that. He did in accepting his 1997 AFI Lifetime Achievement Award.

Deeply focussed

Orson Welles' use of deep focus in *Citizen Kane* impressed editor Wise who emulated the photographic technique in his noirs. Adroit use of lighting allows both foreground and background to be in focus. Welles, a top-notch magician, was not the originator of deep focus. Noir cinematographic genius James Wong Howe used deep focus in *Algiers* 1938.

Filmmakers:
Left to right:
Val Lewton, Mark Robson, and Kirk Douglas from the noir *Champion*.

Ventures with Val

Mark Robson was assistant editor to Wise on *Citizen Kane*. Both progressed to directing noirs via the RKO horrors produced by Val Lewton. Wise did *The Body Snatcher* 1945 and Robson directed *Isle of the Dead* 1945 and *Bedlam* 1946. His best noir was *Champion*.

Censors are funny

The Motion Picture Daily December 5, 1947, reported funny business on pages 1 and 4. *Born to Kill* was among fourteen films banned by the Hays Office from reissue. The others were *Shoot to Kill* 1947, *The Killers* 1946, *They Made Me a Killer* 1946, *Dillinger* 1945, *Roger Touhy, Gangster* 1945, *The Racket Man* 1944, *This Gun for Hire* 1943, *Ellery Queen and the Murder Ring* 1941, *The Last Gangster* 1937, *The Racketeers* 1930, *Me Gangster* 1928, *Ladies of the Mob* 1928, and *Gang War* 1928.

The funny business was that only the titles were banned by the Motion Picture Association for reissue, but a technicality banned the entire films' reissue.

Page 4 of the *Motion Picture Daily* explained that the Hays Office claimed that, by law, any reissue under a different name had to include the former title in the same size print as the new title. Thus, any reissue under the new title would contain the old title and hence was banned.

Forever Am$#r

The MPA gave a reprieve to the title of a film then in production, *Forever Amber* 1947. "Fairness dictated that the new provisions not having been in existence when current releases went into production these pictures should not be so governed." I know you are thinking is the naughty word *forever* or *amber*. While you should not stare too deeply into the abyss of the censorial mind, there seems to be little historical evidence of amber having naughty associations to include the word in a ban on "titles associated in the public mind with material, characters, or occupations unsuitable for the screen." The ban related to the source novel that had sexual interludes. The public would not have read the novel nor of its ban in some states. But best to mention we know the title is naughty while we are taking no action. Censors are funny.

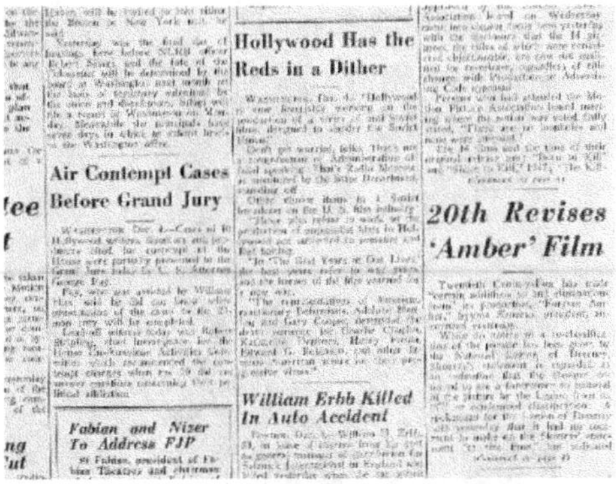

Hollywood Has the Reds in a Dither

Air Contempt Cases Before Grand Jury

20th Revises 'Amber' Film

William Erbb Killed In Auto Accident

Fabian and Nizer To Address FJP

The Cold War waged across the front page of the *Motion Picture Daily* of December 5, 1947, surely a collector's item. One report informed how U.S. Attorney George Fay had presented, to a Grand Jury, accusations of contempt by the Hollywood Ten who had refused to answer House Un-American Activities Committee (HUAC) questions about their political alliances. The ten were Alvah Bessie, Herbert Biberman, Lester Cole, Edward Dmytryk, Ring Lardner Jr., John Howard Lawson, Albert Maltz, Samuel Ornitz, Adrian Scott, and Dalton Trumbo.

Writers were over-represented: Bessie, Biberman (also a director), Cole, Howard, Lardner, Lawson, Maltz, and Trumbo. Dmytryk was a director and Scott was a producer. German playwright/director Bertolt Brecht fled the country after giving sarcastic evidence to the HUAC. Brecht predicted he would have been the eleventh man and he went to Switzerland.

The ten were imprisoned for six months to a year. Dmytryk escaped early by naming names of fellow communists. He was able to resume his career. Dmytryk blamed Scott and Trumbo for making him put Commie stuff in his otherwise pristine movies. Scott produced the Dmytryk-directed classics, *Murder, My Sweet* 1944, and *Crossfire* 1947, as well as the profitable *Cornered* 1945. Trumbo wrote the Dmytryk-directed *Tender Comrade* 1943 that the HUAC decided was Communist propaganda. No doubt they figured that from the title. That revelation must have shocked *Tender Comrade* conservative star Ginger Rogers.

For comic relief, the newspaper made fun of Radio Moscow broadcasting, "Those who refuse to work on the production of imperialist films in Hollywood are subjected to pressure and Red-baiting." Sloganeering aside, the Moscow media had a point. Moscow's other jibe was hyperbolic: "The representatives of American reactionary Bohemians, Adolphe Menjou and Gary Cooper, demanded the death sentence for Charlie Chaplin, Katharine Hepburn, Henry Fonda, Edward G. Robinson, and other famous American actors for their progressive views." Menjou and Cooper as bohemians was laughable. As for death sentences, studios did threaten to kill off Hepburn's career when cinema owners named her box-office poison in 1938. Rehabilitated with the 1940 hit *The Philadelphia Story,* Hepburn's career strode forth. The HUAC hounded comedic genius Chaplin out of the country in 1952. Robinson was graylisted for three years.

Good lines

Born to Kill is based on the 1942 novel by 21-year-old James Dunn. The author did not participate in the scriptwriting, but he gained credit for the noirs *The Unfaithful* 1947, *Affair in Trinidad* 1952, and *Over-Exposed* 1956. He was a television scriptwriter for the noir-influenced series *Mickey Spillane's Mike Hammer* 1957-59, *77 Sunset Strip* 1958-64, and *Checkmate* 1960-62.

The novel is more blackly humorous than the film. You could envisage the lines of the film played for morbid laughs. But I believe director Robert Wise made the correct call in having the actors stress the irony. So too with changing the title from *Deadlier Than the Male* so we could enjoy Trevor's character development without prejudice. The novel did centralize Trevor's role more.

Quotable quotes:

Claire Trevor: I must warn you, though, liquor makes me nosy. I've been known to ask all sorts of personal questions after four cocktails.

Elisha Cook Jr: 'Sallright. I've been known to tell people to mind their own business. Cold sober, too.

Lawrence Tierney: I've got a dame on my mind - and she's dead. That's plenty for me.

Esther Howard to Trevor: You're the coldest iceberg of a woman I ever saw, and the rottenest inside. I've seen plenty, too. I wouldn't trade places with you if they sliced me into little pieces.

Walter Slezak: As you grow older, you'll discover that life is very much like coffee: the aroma is always better than the actuality.

Tierney: Oh, I see. You cross the tracks on May Day with a basket of goodies for the poor slum kid, but back you scoot - and fast - to your own neck o' the woods. Don't you?
Trevor: I wouldn't say that.
Tierney: No, you wouldn't say it . . . but that's the way it is.

Cook: You can't just go around killing people whenever the notion strikes you - it's not feasible.

The verdict: *Born to Kill* is a film noir classic: ★★★★★

2005

Chapter 14: Stolen baguette goes stale

The Hollywood producers of *The Long Night* 1947 tried to search for and destroy all copies of the French original, the poetic-realist film *Le jour se lève* 1939. Having classic films destroyed is not so easy as British courts found when they ordered the destruction of *Nosferatu: A Symphony of Horror* 1922 because the courts deemed it a Dracula clone.

Trivia

Le jour se lève translates to *Daybreak* which would have been a snazzier title than Hollywood's *The Long Night*. The RKO producers did not want a reminder of their foul practice of film burning, the capital punishment the London court imposed on *Nosferatu*. It looked as if RKO had done a better job with *Le jour se lève*, but copies resurfaced during the 1950s and, today the French film is far more likely to appear at a classic film festival than *The Long Night*. That's karma for you.

Jean Gabin, the star of *Daybreak,* had come to Hollywood to make *Moontide* 1942 with Ida Lupino. It had flourishes of poetic realism, a movement in 1930s French film in which people on the margins of society were partially represented in lyrical metaphors.

Gabin starred in a French movie *Pépé le Moko* 1937 that used poetic realism as did the American copy *Algiers* 1938 with Charles Boyer in the Gabin role. Americans were not novices in consuming poetic realism, but they didn't fancy the taste of *The Long Night*.

It is hard to get in the groove of the movie early. First, a narrator talks to us in folksy Americana and introduces us to blind war veteran Elisha Cook Jr. who leads us upstairs to a murder amid expressionist noir photography. Realism and poetry clash in *The Long Night* as they never did in *Algiers* or *Moontide*. We hear contrivances and see the wires, jarring interruptions to the enjoyment of the movie about a police siege of the protagonist living on the top floor of a residential brownstone in a working-class urban area.

Male leads, the taciturn Henry Fonda and the verbose Vincent Price, are dull characters who struggle to maintain viewer interest. Broadway prodigy Barbara Bel Geddes and 1930s' star Ann Dvorak do better, and we filmgoers wish them well in their pursuit of joy. As Fonda's shy love interest, Bel Geddes displays a quiet naturalness, suited to cinema, and a contrast to Dvorak's jaded cynicism, also suited to the big screen. The dogs in Price's magic act were excellent, but I failed to catch their names among the credits.

After Elisha Cook Jr.'s appearance at the start, we await his return, as the blind veteran could have a compelling back story. Fonda showed he was kind to children and cats but that did not do it for us. Cook's was just one of the working-class voices raised in support of Fonda who mistook loyal members of his community for rubberneckers. The film picks up at the 1hr:16m mark when these scenes unfold.

With all those cops present, one of them could have told talented composer Dmitri Tiomkin to turn down the music. Cinematographer Sol Polito (*Sorry Wrong Number* 1948) does a sterling job on the crowd scenes. The good bits lasted only a couple of minutes, after which normal melodrama resumed.

Attendees who did not fall asleep at test screenings must have requested a happy ending.

We never found out how Elisha Cook Jr. became blind.

The Player

Plenty to see: Ann Dvorak, smart doggies working for a ham (Vincent Price) and the obscure reference of a "no vacancy" sign.

In 1936, Ann Dvorak delivered a great Hollywood line outside a movie. She wrote to Funk and Wagnalls' *The Literary Digest*: "My fake name is properly pronounced vor'shack."

People born with the name Dvorak vigorously proclaimed her pronunciation was wrong. Such protests were inappropriate. When Hollywood indulged in the fundamental ritual of making up a name, surely, they could decide pronunciation of their fraudulent moniker.

Charles E. Funk reduced the humor of Ms. Dvorak quoting how to pronounce her made-up name by leaving out the word "fake" in his 1936 book. But recounting the incensed reactions of authentic Dvoraks made up for omission.

Funk Charles E. *What's The Name, Please? A guide to the Correct Pronunciation of Current Prominent Names*, New York Funk & Wagnalls, 1936, page 54.

Dvorak was born Anna McKim.

Ann Dvorak was a child actor in silents, and, at 19 years old, had her first adult part as a lead in the gangster proto-noir *Scarface* 1932. She was in the excellent crime drama *Three on a Match* with Bette Davis and Joan Blondell. She was in *G-Men* 1935 (about government agents) which Warners made to placate censors who despised successful gangster films. Chicago banned it to prove yet again that censors are funny.

Dvorak's 1935 court case against Warners preceded the famous Bette Davis one of two years' later. Both actors lost but Davis got better roles while Dvorak performed well in B-pictures. Dvorak's last film was the excellent noir Western *The Secret of Convict Lake* 1951.

Well played, Ms Vor'shack.

The Player

Justice:
Henry Fonda is the right man for *The Wrong Man*.

Celebrated actor Henry Fonda had a mediocre average in noirs, scoring one out of three. Hitchcock's *The Wrong Man* 1956 was excellent with Fonda as a jazz musician wrongly charged with robbery. The movie is based on a true story and Hitchcock always privileged suspense over mystery, so he did not mind giving the plot away in the film's title.

Fonda's other foray into noir was in the melodrama *Daisy Kenyon* 1947.

Despite the presence of Joan Crawford and Dana Andrews, this film bored me, but not as much as do the critics who earnestly deny it is film noir. Enough already, what is that still above, chopped liver? I do not know why I am channelling a 1940s' Jewish comedian, but you get the picture.

During the age of noir, 1940-59, Fonda was a fine versatile actor in the drama *The Grapes of Wrath* 1940, the comedy *The Lady Eve* 1941, the Western *The Ox-Bow Incident* 1943, the comedy drama *Mister Roberts* 1955, and the legal drama *Twelve Angry Men* 1957. Maybe noir was not his thing.

Henry was the father of actors, Jane and Peter Fonda. At 87, Jane is still righting wrongs. Or trying to. What more can you ask of someone?

The verdict: *The Long Night.* 

Chapter 15: Gangster weirdness

The Gangster 1947 is weird un, while I can never get my head around why you would call a main character in a crime noir *Flaxy Martin* 1949.

We knew *The Gangster* and *Flaxy Martin* would not be noir classics: Cook's name appeared on the posters. By 1947, he had lost the Jr. but he found it again in 1949.

Despite the poster credit, Cook appears in only one scene in *The Gangster* . He plays a one-name character Oval, a trigger-happy hired punk, stylishly dressed in gangster chic. As with many scenes in the movies, it was all talk, no action. Cook was among an array of talent in this B-picture that was too symbolic for its own good when you could not work out what the symbols were on about.

The lead character played by Barry Sullivan also has one name, and what a doozy it is, Shubunka. The Japanese-bred goldfish shubunkin is an unlikely reference. Bunker for the emotionally unavailable gangster might be closer. I reckon bunkum fits best.

The support players in the movie include Akim Tamiroff, John Ireland, Shelley Winters, Charles McGraw, and Sheldon Leonard.

The film is based on a novel by Daniel Fuchs (*Criss Cross* 1949) who also wrote the screenplay with uncredited blacklisted Dalton Trumbo. The play in screenplay is relevant here as the plot unfolds like a meaningful drama that challenges the audience to unravel it. I failed.

The Verdict: *The Gangster* 

The producers of *The Gangster* were the King brothers, Frank and Morris. The third brother in King Brothers Production was Hyman.

The brothers, born Kozinsky, with sister Nettie, built up a small slot-machine empire in Los Angeles in the 1920s.

In the 1930s, the Brothers invented a slot machine that played moving pictures, but they needed product for it. They teamed up with Cecil B. De Mille who was infringing an exclusive contract by joining the bros. De Mille gave them nothing and the Kozinsky brothers were slighted. In what reads like a tongue -in-cheek account, a contemporary journalist explained the slight.

"They have a racing stable, which entitles them to respect from any movie executive. At Hollywood Park they have a box between Louis B. Mayer's and Frank Capra's."

"So, we had to go ahead," Morris, says, "or else we would have looked cheap to Mayer and Capra, because we'd told them about it."

Brady T. *Kozinsky Brothers Muscled Into the Movies to Get Even With De Mille, New York Times,* Oct 12, 1941, Section X, page 4.

The slot mechanics would show De Mille. They would take him on in his own game of movie production.

Their first movie, *Paper Bullets* 1941 cost $23,000 to make, was filmed in six days, and Poverty Row studio Producers Releasing Corporation distributed. Poverty Row referred as much to modest figures on balance sheet as humble Hollywood addresses.

Future noir star Alan Ladd had a bit part. Ladd displayed that breezy style that made him a star after 10 years of hard slog in bit parts, often uncredited.

Prolific crime and Western actor Joan Woodbury were cast as female lead. "There was only one chair in the office (Morris Kozinsky said). 'She didn't care and sat down on the floor. Right then I knew she was a trouper and I signed her up.'"

Brady T. *NYT*, Oct 12, 1941.

The ultra-B crime movie *Paper Bullets* grossed $200,000. It is an enjoyable film that addresses questions of social injustice and political corruption.

Seeking Linda:

Teenage actor/ singer Linda Ware was good in the role of nightclub singer Donna Andrews in *Paper Bullets.* Ware had spent part of her life in an orphanage after being abandoned by her father. He tried to regain custody when she had the makings of a star. Ware was 13 years old when cast in a leading role in *The Star Maker* 1939 starring Bing Crosby.

Struttin' her stuff

Linda Ware gave a good rendition of the 1917 jazz standard *Darktown Strutters' Ball* in *The Star Maker*. She was emulating the legends Sophie Tucker and Ella Fitzgerald in performing that song.

Despite credible performances in two movies, Ware never made a third.

What happened to her is a mystery, apart from her death, aged 50, in Las Vegas.

I am the owner of the above autograph from the *Jimmie Brown Collection*.

If anyone has more information on Ms. Ware, please email me through the address in the opening credits of this book.

Trivia

Australian pop band, Ted Mulry Gang, had a hit with *Darktown Strutters' Ball* in 1976. I saw them play the song thirty years later in the City of Moreton Bay.

The King Brothers worked with Oscar winning scriptwriter Phillip Yordan (*Broken Lance* 1954).

Yordan wrote the noirs *When Strangers Marry* 1944, the surprise hit *Dillinger* 1945, and *Suspense* 1946.

The King Brothers produced the noir classic *Gun Crazy* 1950. *Paper Bullets* failed to make Linda Ware a star but it helped the King Brothers assist other noir creatives.

I do not get it when they put noir credits in a flowery font. I mean, come on, that looks the font for a 1930s screwball comedy.

Unlike *The Gangster*, *Flaxy Martin* starts off with a bang, actually a few bangs, followed by an assassin running from the scene.

Dial A for assassin:
Bit player, left, rings the police.
Virginia Mayo, below, plots.

A frantic call to the police reports the murder. The noir aesthetic of the phone call deserves more credit. Directors, cinematographers, and set designers loved that phone call. They went to a deal of trouble to maximize the impact of what would end up as less than a minute of screen time.

Improbabilities plague the plot of *Flaxy Martin*, the name for starters. Flaxy is a singer. The least they could have done was to have her perform in a basement dive called the *Linen Closet*. Not that I am complaining about Virginia Mayo not singing. There was far too much inappropriate singing in 1940s film noir. Mayo started her career in comedies and musicals before she teamed up with Warners, specialists in medium-budget noirs. She plays a callous femme fatale and there is little depth to her character. She does warn her sucker Zachary Scott that she loves money as much as him. This is before we realize she is a baddie. We can have a chuckle recalling that line when we find out. Mayo had a riveting turn in the noir *White Heat* 1949 in which she played the sadistic wife of psychotic gangster James Cagney.

Zachary Scott was a top actor in noir. He had a pleasant soothing voice that contrasted well with all the traditional mayhem he endured in his noir films. In *Flaxy Martin*, he must face the consequences of all the silly assessments and decisions his lawyer character makes that leave viewers little choice but to think he is as dumb as a box of rocks.

So many guns, so few brains, to quote Phillip Marlowe. Above are Mayo and Scott. At right are Cook, Scott, and the librarian Dorothy Malone still in books after *The Big Sleep*.

At 40 minutes in, feisty good gal Dorothy Malone appears, and I feel apprehensive about the future of femme fatale Mayo (bad gal). Wouldn't you know it, insecure villain Cook places in peril the destined-for-romance couple, Malone and Scott. Cook explained feebly how he tracked them listening into police calls before following every lead. This was just after a cop had explained how they received so many dead-end tips.

Cook never explained the mystery of why he kept calling attorney Scott "Shamus". Elisha was in enough noirs to know a shamus was a PI. Scripter David Lang became a prolific writer of TV Westerns, but he shares the blame for the sloppiness of the plot.

"You been pretty loose with your big talk, ain'tcha. Well, I ain't taking it no more," Elisha says. Where have we heard that sort of threat before? Oh yair, from Elisha in half a dozen other movies. "You and me's gonna take a little ride." Please, Elisha, stop, shoot us if you must, but shut up with the gangster jive. *Flaxy Martin* is the only movie with Elisha Cook Jr. that we wish we had seen and heard less of him.

Good line

We had to wait until the end for the one particularly good line.

Douglas Kennedy: She's a great kid. You can always trust her to double-cross you.

The verdict: *Flaxy Martin*
★★⯪☆☆

Chapter 16: Monroe and Cook: what a team!

Quite the coincidence that Hollywood moguls, producers, directors, and critics disparaged the acting talents of the two great Hollywood beauties of the 1940s and 1950s: Hedy Lamarr and Marilyn Monroe.

Director John Cromwell and male lead Charles Boyer congratulated each other for extracting what they regarded as a barely adequate performance from Lamarr in the proto-noir *Algiers* 1938. Yet Lamarr lights up the screen except for a couple of scenes that could have been better edited.

Billy Wilder, who directed Monroe in *The Seven Year Itch* 1955 and *Some Like It Hot* 1959, said getting a performance from her was like pulling teeth. Yet Monroe was a significant contributor to Wilder's lauded great comedies as well as to *Gentlemen Prefer Blondes* 1953 and *How to Marry a Millionaire* 1953.

In the noir *Don't Bother to Knock* 1952 Monroe consorted with the man of a thousand fails Elisha Cook Jr.to steal the movie from stars Richard Widmark and Anne Bancroft. It was as if Widmark and Bancroft were foils to set up the charged interchanges between uncle Cook and niece Monroe.

Widmark, playing commitment-phobic pilot Jed Towers, does have clever patter with Willis B. Bouchey playing a bartender.

Good lines

Jed Towers: Seventy-eight percent of the pilots in Skyway Airlines are married. Ya' see, you get married, you become a statistic.

Joe the Bartender: Stay single, and you wind up talkin' to bartenders.

Bouchey was a bit player in the good noirs *Deadline - U.S.A.* 1952, *Pickup on South Street* 1953, and *The Big Heat* 1953.

Monroe plays a mentally-ill woman, recovering from the trauma of the post-war death of her partner, a former air force pilot. Uncle Eddie, a humble elevator operator, tries to help her recover through work as a babysitter. He is unsure if his niece has conquered her illness.

Nell Forbes: I haven't had earrings on for three years. All through high school, I never had a dress to wear out at night. A month ago, I came here on a bus. I'd walk down the street, look in the beautiful stores. Eddie calls it "window-wishing". Then I got this job tonight.

Bibliophile: Monroe reads one of husband Arthur Miller's plays. The 1950 play is an adaptation and modernization of Henrik Ibsen's 1882 drama in which vested interests and narrow-minded citizens deny a flawed doctor's findings of water polution.

No records exist of Marilyn Monroe or her husband Arthur Miller taking an I.Q. test. Monroe's I.Q. in the upper genius category of 160-168 is an urban myth. Her library of hundreds of books is not mythical.

Teenager: Norma is at Santa Catalina, LA County.

Smarts: High-school dropout Norma Jeane Baker was one smart cookie who later in life took classes at the University of California, Los Angeles.

In a previous book on film noir, I coined the term *pulchriphobia*, for powerful Hollywood men's fear of a beautiful woman whom they had to demean, and, in some cases, destroy.

Critic Julian Fox wrote, "Marilyn Monroe is not very convincing as the babysitter. She ought to stick to glamor roles" Elsewhere in the review he says Monroe is "the hottest thing" since Jean Harlow.

Fox J. *Marilyn Monroe Stars In New film at Globe,*
Brooklyn Eagle July 19, 1952, page 14.

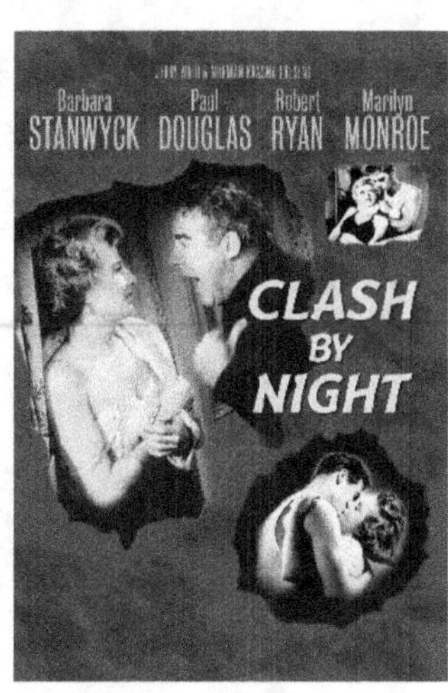

Brooklyn Eagle critic Julian Fox was oblivious of the fact that four of the five Monroe films released between 1950-52 were noirs. Her breakout role was in the heist noir *The Asphalt Jungle* 1950. A minor but impressive role in the noir satire *All About Eve* 1950 followed. Gritty seaside noir *Clash By Night* 1952 preceded *Don't Bother to Knock*. Monroe does not play a "glamour girl" in any of these four films.

During the five years before she entered *The Asphalt Jungle*, Monroe exhausted two studio contracts, appearing in two small parts and a lead in the low-budget musical romance *Ladies of the Chorus* 1948. The director was future B-noir baron, Phil Karlson (*Scandal Sheet* 1952, *Kansas City Confidential* 1952, *99 River Street* 1953, *Hell's Island* 1955, and *The Brothers Rico* 1957). In *Ladies of the Chorus*, Monroe sang and danced, well rather than exceptionally. She had only been learning for two years. Monroe's acting was reasonable but the performances of some supports were inadequate. The film had a limited releas. Columbia did not renew her contract. Colombia's 1952 re-release was half-hearted as she had returned to Fox which had released her in 1947. *Ladies of the Chorus* is a watchable film with its story of mother and daughter burlesque performers and their interaction with a wealthy family.The fabulous Mr. Karlson filmed the movie in 10 days. *Ladies of the Chorus* Cinematographer Frank Redman captured the noir mise-en-scènes of the TV courtroom drama *Perry Mason* 1957-66.

Photograph: *American Cinematographer*

What a great year was 1950 for film noir satires on the performing arts with the release of *Sunset Boulevard* on Hollywood cinema and *All About Eve* on Broadway theater. Both movies abound with witty lines. Here is one from Monroe, the butt is a theater critic played admirably by George Sanders. To set the scene, Addison DeWitt (Sanders) is grooming acting hopeful Claudia Casswell (Monroe) and they are talking with cloying theater groupie Eve Harrington (Anne Baxter).

Eve: I am aftraid Mr. DeWitt would find me boring before too long.

Claudia: You won't bore him, Honey. You won't even get a chance to talk.

It was ironic that an early Monroe role had her being prized for her beauty and overlooked regarding her intellect. Throughout her career Monroe played the idiot savant well but it took a toll personally.

Bette Davis is the protagonist and antagonist in *All About Eve*. It is fitting that I quote Margot Channing in a response to Hugh Marlowe.

Marlowe: (Lloyd Richards): A Hollywood movie star just arrived.

Margo: (Davis): Shucks, and I sent my autograph book to the cleaner.

Asphalt absurdism:

In *The Asphalt Jungle*, Monroe plays the childlike mistress of a crooked lawyer (Louis Calhern) bankrolling a heist and double-crossing the robbers.

Her stream-of-consciousness rave of going on a Cuban holiday is a stark contrast to the dire events unfolding after the robbery goes bad: "Imagine me on this beach here in my green bathing suit. Yipe! I almost bought a white one the other day, but it wasn't quite extreme enough. I mean, don't get me wrong, if I really went in for the extreme extreme, I woulda' bought a French one. Run for your lives, girls, the fleet's in. Oh, Uncle Lon, am I excited. Yipe!"

That is excellent scripting from Ben Maddow, expertly delivered by Monroe.

Maddow was nominated for an Academy Award and blacklisted from 1952-60.

Defiant:

A cop arrives to shake her false alibi shielding her lover Uncle Lon. Monroe reacts defiantly. "Haven't you bothered me enough, you big banana head?"

That is excellent scripting from Ben Maddow, assuredly delivered by Monroe.

Maddow was nominated for an Academy Award and blacklisted from 1952-60.

Huston J. *An Open Book*, page 287.

John Huston directed Monroe's last completed film, *The Misfits* 1961. The director confirmed her habitual lateness to the set that her husband Arthur Miller said was due to her obsession with lots of sleep to look her best. Her nightly and daily ritual involced taking downers and uppers. Drug addiction was Monroe's core problem. Huston said Monroe, on a good day, could reach into her method acting training and become a character. Monroe wrecked the financials of *The Misfits* as well her marriage to the screenwriter Miller. Huston predicted tragedy for her but he believed her death in 1962 was from an accidental overdose. He quoted French writer/ philosopher Jean-Paul Sartre who said Monroe was the best female actor working in the 1950s.

The establishing scene of Monroe and Cook riding to the floor where she will baby-sit is beautifully handled by the actors, director Roy Baker, and cinematographer Lucien Ballard. Neither Uncle Eddie nor niece Nell convinces us as they try to reassure each other the baby-sitting gig could lead to good times. Something is way off, but we viewers cannot deduce what the issue is.

Eddie gives Nell the idea that New York has many young men. She can find one to help her over the loss of her partner. Wearing her employer's jewellery, exotic perfume, and negligee – kimono, Eddie calls it –, she invites jilted pilot, Jed, to her hotel room.

Two harrowing scenes happen in the room. First Jed rescues the child hanging out a window with Nell threatening to push her. The second is when Jed sees the wrist scars of Nell's self-harm. The subdued action of the film, panned by critics, returns big dividends in these scenes.

Uncle Eddie turns out not to be the consistently nice guy we thought he was. Turns out he can be as psychologically abusive as Nell's parents were.

An attractive scene has the child peering through the keyhole of her bedroom door. The English director might have been watching European arthouse the night before the shoot. We see the purpose of the scene when violence ensues, and the child cries off-camera. Neat sequence.

The verdict: *Don't Bother to Knock* ★★★★☆

I, THE JURY (1953)

has been restored by
UCLA FILM & TELEVISION ARCHIVE
in conjunction with
PKL PICTURES LTD
and
ROMULUS FILMS LIMITED

Laboratory services
ROUNDABOUT ENTERTAINMENT
THE UCLA DIGITAL LAB
AUDIO MECHANICS
SIMON DANIEL SOUND

Special Thanks to
CONNIE ELLIOT
NICK VARLEY

I have always depended on the kindness of strangers to restore classic film noir. But I have to say I am surprised they bothered restoring *I, the Jury* 1953, a film in which Elisha Cook Jr. has an uncredited role.

The movie starts off promisingly with the murder of a war veteran who has a prosthetic arm. Almost immediately, we realize that we are about to watch one of the worst acting performances on film. Newcomer Biff Elliot plays Mickey Spillane's Mike Hammer, and the perpetually angry man grabs the limb and swears he will avenge the murder of the man who gave his right arm for him during World War II. Alas, poor Jack. No, it is not camp, it is bad bad bad. Not bad bad bad that it's good. Just bad bad bad.

I, the Jury is not a total loss. The cinematography was by John Alton and the music by Franz Waxman. They can't save the picture, only their reputations.

As a civic service to save you pain, I report that Cook as Bobo enters at 27:50. An entertaining minute follows as intellectually challenged Bobo explains how he has given up numbers-racket couriering for bee-keeping in a cardboard hive on a tenement roof. He next appears at 53:05. He has a job as a Santa Claus, and he has bought a queen bee. "queen bees don't need no king," he tells Hammer. I won't say what happened to Bobo except that it was not goodwill to one man.

Birth of an auteur:

Young Stanley Kubrick's third film was a noir, *The Killing* 1956. He is pictured with the lead, Sterling Hayden.

Kubrick was a still photographer before he moved into movies. The structure of film noir tamed his brash imagination, and he was able to leap from *The Killing* to become one of the world's great directors. One of reasons for the success of *The Killing* was his astuteness in casting, He had to convince his backers to hire Hayden who had not set the cinematic word alight since *The Asphalt Jungle* of 1950. His other inspired choices were B-listers Marie Windsor and Cook.

French deviation: Have a good look at the French poster of *The Killing.* See who supports Hayden: Gray and Edwards. But caricatures of Cook and Windsor are pictured.

The French loved their film noir. They loved femme fatale Windsor, and they loved perennial loser Cook.

The lobby card below was intent on giving the plot away. Spoilers!

I regard Cook's role in *The Killing* as the third exceptional performance of his lengthy career after *The Maltese Falcon* and *The Big Sleep*. Cast without the Jr. Cook relished the big-boy screen time, though he was still noir's favorite patsy married to the unfaithful Marie Windsor. His is the biggest role I have seen Cook play.

Personal failings and the whimsy of Fate combine to destroy George Peatty (Cook). With his weak character, poor choices, and being supernatural Fate's plaything, Cook has the more traditional role of the protagonist in a tragedy than Sterling Hayden who gets kicked in the teeth by Fate repeatedly, just because. George is ripe for humiliation.

From his earliest scenes, we viewers have a pitiful sympathy for George as he tries to win back his wife Sherry's love that we suspect was never there in the first place. We know it is going to end badly for George and can only shake our heads when he reveals the heist plan to his wife. Sherry is having an affair with Val Cannon (Vince Edwards, television's future fictional surgeon *Ben Casey* 1961-66. Val's motto in *The* Killing is "first, do plenty of harm." George blabbing to Sherry starts the heist falling apart.

Critics have suggested the Windsor character, Sherry Peatty, in *The Killing* is a Kubrick misogynist fantasy. Peatty is a greedy conniving disloyal woman whose scheming leads to the downfall of three men. It seems like a sexist caricature, but an unredeemed evil minor character, male or female, is an effective trope in noir. In Kubrick's work, beginning with *Killer's Kiss*, toxic male misogyny has been a theme.

The Verdict: *The Killing* ★★★★☆

Chapter 17: Murdering two genres

Cook's next noirs were poor interpretations of film noir and horror though both Republic B-pictures had connections to much better movies.

Elisha Cook Jr. does okay in *Accused of Murder* 1956 when he comes on at 41:12 to play recovering wino Whitey Pollock, who gives murder information of questionable reliability. That tall copper beside him is indeed one of our favorite noir villains, Lee Van Cleef, he of the late fame in spaghetti Westerns. Van Cleef's boss to the left is David Brian. Despite Cook and Van Cleef, this color movie is a noir on antidepressants. If you last to the end, you might need them. Neither the bright vibrant colors nor the sets scream noir.

The highlight is when Lee Van Cleef realizes his boss is falling in love with a nightclub singer, Vera Ralston. Former Olympic figure skater Ralston leads the credits, but she only appears in a handful of scenes. Given her mediocre acting and dull persona, we see why. Beside David Brian is Frank Puglia, a support in 150 movies. In *Accused of Murder* he dispenses banal homespun wisdom. We wonder why no one shoots him.

The screenwriter

Three gangsters: Edward G. Robinson (actor) W.R Burnett (writer) and Mervyn Le Roy (director) combined for *Little Caesar*, a hit and model for proto-noir gangster films of the 1930s Great Depression.

Little Caesar was based on Burnett's 1929 novel. You can buy a first edition for USD15,000.

The connection of *Accused of Murder* to better movies came through screenwriter W.R. Burnett (*Little Caesar* 1931, *High Sierra* 1940, *This Gun for Hire* 1942, noir Western *Yellow Sky* 1948, and *The Asphalt Jungle* 1950). *Accused of Murder* was based on Burnett's novel *Vanity Row* 1952. "They paid me a lot of money for it. They paid me to write the script. I wrote the script just like the book; I got my money and left."
The studio made changes.
"The whole goddamned show went out the window," Burnett said.
McGilligan P. *Backstory: interviews with screenwriters of Hollywood's golden age*, University of California Press 1986, page 77. (Ken Mate was co-interviewer of Burnett)

As an aside, Burnett claimed a nickname for Republic was Repulsive. The problem with *Accused of Murder* was that it was not repulsive enough. The dull ambience of scenes was distant from Burnett's literary works admired by his co-scriptwriter on *High Sierra* John Huston. "There are moments of reality in his books that are overpowering, had me breaking into a sweat." Huston J. 1980, page 78.
Burnett's description of his theme for Little Caesar could apply to his other crime epics. "I was reaching for a gutter Macbeth". McGilligan P. 1986, page 57.
Unfortunately, Accused *of Murder* was signifying nothing, without the sound and fury.
Burnett was used to Hollywood diluting his work. He had a "beef with Sam Briskin producer of *The Whole Town's Talking* 1936, based on Burnett's story *Jail Breaker*.
Briskin: Why don't you write a story that's got a good finish on it?"
Burnett: Why did you buy it? ("I never did take any of that crap from Hollywood.")
McGilligan P. 1986, page 63.

The verdict: *Accused of Murder* ★★☆☆☆

Burnett and John Huston have different versions of how Humphrey Bogart got the lead in *High Sierra*, the first step to Hollywood stardom for the 40-year-old journeyman. The Burnett version is more colorful and more accurate.

First the short Huston take: "Paul Muni (*Scarface* 1932) was offered the lead, and I was pleased when he turned it down and Humphrey Bogart got to do it. Before this picture Bogie was well down the list at Warners. *High Sierra* marked a turning point in his career." Huston J. 1980, page 78.

Now the extended Burnett version:

"John (Huston), who belted the grape a little now and then, was at one of those big Hollywood cocktail parties with Paul Muni, and he didn't like Muni. Warners had bought the book for Muni.

"John got a little loaded and told Muni what he thought of him as an actor. So, Muni waited until the script came to him, and he turned it down because Huston was the writer.

"So, Jack Warner said to Huston, "Get Burnett. Get Burnett and let him work on the script with you, and if Muni comes up with any objections, we'll say, 'For chrissakes, what do you want? We got the author on it."

"Anyway, we got a fine script and gave it to Muni, and Muni turned it down again. You know what happened? Warner fired him.

"I thought the studio was going to collapse that day. Everybody went around saying, "For chrissakes, they fired Muni. He's getting five thousand a week. You can't fire the star." McGilligan P. 1986, page 64.

The eminent noir connections of *Voodoo Island* 1957 stretched back to Frankenstein 1931, steeped in German Expressionism and starring Englishman Boris Karloff who made a career in horror. *Voodoo Island* director Reginald LeBorg was an accomplished B-movie creator whose best noirs were *Destiny* 1944 and *Fall Guy* 1947.

Before *Voodoo Island*, LeBorg directed the B-horror *The Black Sheep* 1956 that gathered a remarkable cast of aging male horror and noir actors – Basil Rathbone, Lon Chaney Jr., John Carradine, Bela Lugosi, and Akim Tamiroff. The film was a financial success.

As for LeBorg, Cook, and Karloff in *Voodoo Island*, let's hope they found time away from filming to relax on the Hawaiian island of Kaua'i where it was filmed.

Horror show: This poster looked good in a cheesy kind of way, but that provoked promises unfulfilled. Karloff plays a myth buster whose attractive research assistant played by Beverly Tyler says, "I'm dull, aren't I?" Karloff should have replied, "Not half as dull as our script."

The eerie sound of the theremin failed to excite the ambience laid low by the dreary inaction of the cast. Elisha Cook (no Jr. In the credits) arrives at the start of the second act to marginally raise the tension. "He's among the dead," Cook says of a zombie the group has brought back to Voodoo Island at Karloff's foolish assistance.

The movie quickly reverts to boring viewers. The spark of a lesbian sub-plot goes nowhere.

LeBorg's next film was better. *The Dalton Girls* 1957 was a feminist Western starring four woman as the children of the dead Dalton gang.

Chapter 18: Dying embers of noir

As film noir limped across the final years of its two-decade run, Cook took part in three more films released in 1957. They were *Chicago Confidential, Plunder Road,* and *Baby Face Nelson.*

Beverly Tyler and a Jr.-less Cook moved from *Voodoo Island* after accepting bit parts in Chicago "islands", still considered in 1957 a prime address for mob movies. This film was promising. Brian Keith was an above-average actor in B-movies. Sidney Salkow was a prolific director of Bs, and cinematographer Kenneth Peach had been shooting pictures since he did early 1930s Laurel and Hardy comedies. With this solid talent on board *Chicago Confidential* was bound to be an entertaining movie.

In keeping with his deleted Jr., Cook plays an old homeless man Candymouth Duggan who finds a gun used by crooked union leaders to kill an honest unionist. Candymouth is central to the frame of another union boss. It is a good turn by Cook as an alcoholic wanting to get back in the union he has been kicked out of because of his drinking. The solving of the crime by vocal analysis was a good twist, well rendered.

Dialog, earnest voiceover, and continual thumping musical intrusions are clichéd but the centrality of unionism and alcoholism into a tale of cops vs. crooks is refreshing.

This film could set a record for close-ups per minute. Taken indiscriminately, they highlight unphotogenic faces. Cook's close-ups are impressive.

The Verdict: *Chicago Confidential* ★ ★ ★

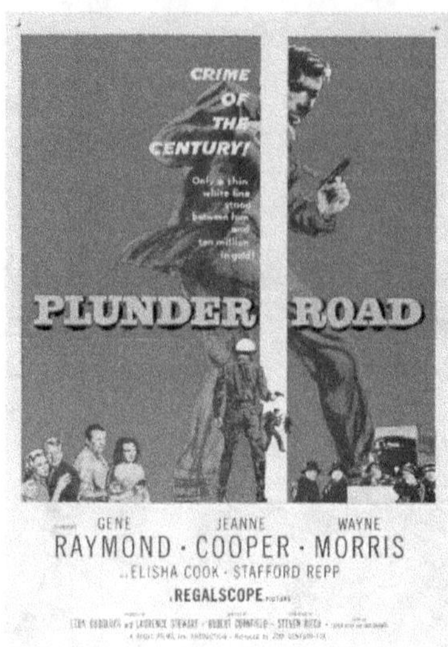

When you embellish your setting into 'crime of the century', viewers suspect they are not about to watch movie of the week. But if we hanged every Hollywood marketer for hyperbole, their ranks would be severely thinned out. Despite the desperate beat-up (in the journalistic sense) *Plunder Road* is a decent B-noir.

After the opening credits, the movie cuts straight to the heist amid driving rain. It has Cook managing an explosive rig he borrowed from a sci-fi film set. The attractive start shows how imagination and day hire of big machinery can overcome budgetary restraint. Toddlers enamored with big mobile machines would have loved it. The thieves rob enough gold to deplete Fort Knox. They need four heavy vehicles to hide it.

We know the rules of noir heists. We settle in to watch the aftermath go pear-shaped. Screenplay writer Steven Ritch has the role of former race-car driver Frankie Chardo who is nervous. In heist-noir structure, nerves predict trouble – for yourself and others. Blaring music alerted us to the disaster ahead.

The film lures us into thinking one of the crew is an informant, but, as with noir tradition, Fate does them in.

The verdict: *Plunder Road* a good cheapie. ★★★

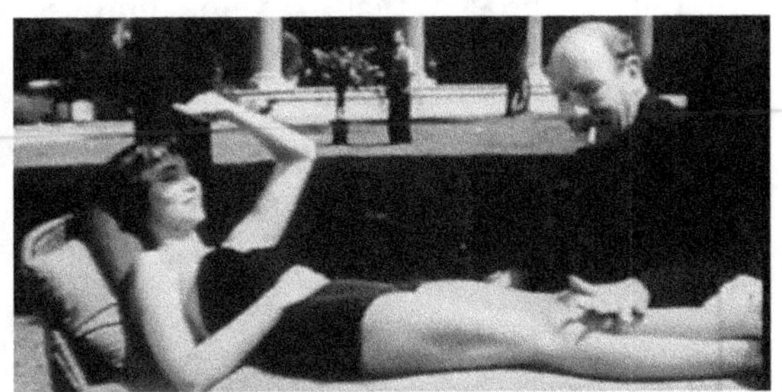

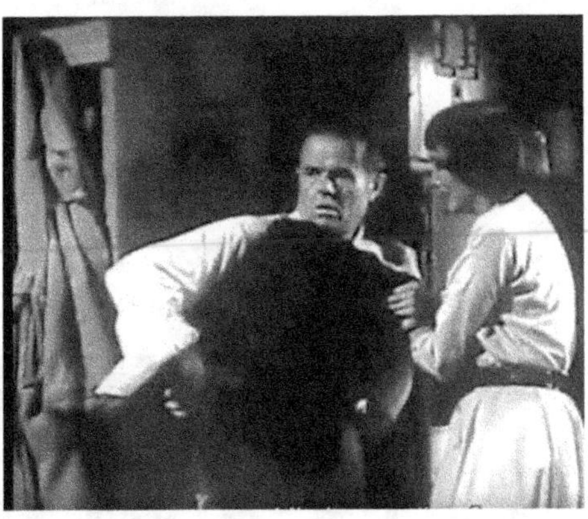

At the end of the second act of *Baby Face Nelson*, the movie killed off the most interesting character, the alcoholic hands-on doctor to the crims, Saunders, played by Cedric Hardwick. At the start of the third act, Elisha Cook Jr. entered as Homer Van Meter. It was not unusual, especially in 1930s screwball comedies, to introduce an accomplished character performer in the third act to insure against viewer fatigue. Both characters are pictured above with Sue Nelson played by Carolyn Jones, remembered fondly as Morticia, matriarch of TV's *The Addams Family* 1964-66.

Replacing one character actor with another is typical of the bureaucratic precision of *Baby Face Nelson*, recreating the visual style of 1930s gangster films while removing the psychological drama at their core. The Hays Office had banned films depicting real life gangsters for two decades and only relented in the mid-fifties. *Baby Face Nelson* producers played it safe with a homage to J. Edgar Hoover and the FBI at the beginning and avoided psychology to show gangsters with whom you do not empathize. In the scene above right, Baby Face Nelson (Mickey Rooney) has thrown Van Meter a bulletproof vest and rained it with slugs to evaluate it. Pretty flashy but no great insight into the character of Baby Face, who shoots at people at every opportunity. This revisionist gangster film worked as a low-budget movie and returned a significant profit. I am unsure how well it stands the test of time, but it does not excite me.

Later in the film Baby Face shoves his vest at Van Meter. "You're gunna wear it. You know why. Coz you're yeller." Both crooks end up dead.

The verdict: Baby Face Nelson ★★☆☆☆

Chapter 19: Two neo-noirs

Noir changed its wardrobe over the 20 years of its lifespan. Styles overlapped their dominant eras, and previous styles did not disappear, but four subgenres are discernible: PI noir 1940 to 1948, woman-centric noir 1945-54, police procedurals 1948-56, and heist noir 1950-59.

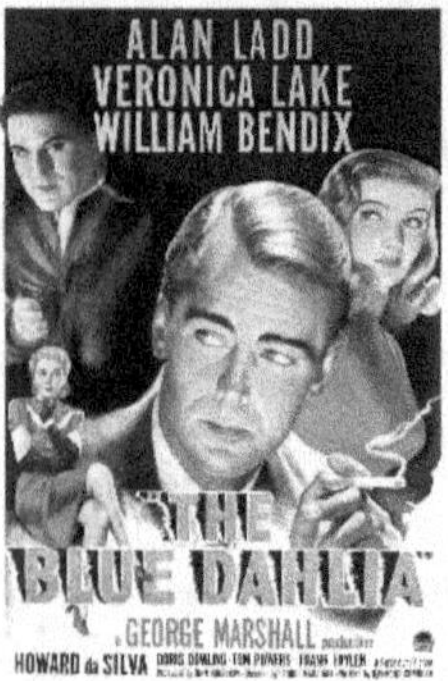

PI noir: 1946

Woman-centric: 1950

Police procedural: 1954

Heist noir: 1957

Noir failed to innovate in the 1950s, and its stylistics and craftspeople migrated to the developing medium of television - voracious but less demanding than film. Cook was among the émigrés.

The Life and Legend of Wyatt Earp: *The Equalizer, 1957*
With Hugh O'Brian

Perry Mason: *The Case of the Pint-Sized Client* 1958
With James Anderson

Peter Gunn: *The Long Long Ride* 1960

Baby Face Nelson was Cook's last noir between 1940-59. With noir's historical and stylistic connections to horror, I mention Cook's 1959 cult favorite *House on Haunted Hill*, at right. The director was William Castle who did the good noir ultracheapie When *Strangers Marry* 1944.

"""

Two neo-noirs, *The Outfit* and *Hammett* form a retrospective of Cook's noir career. He has bit parts in both, but the first places him with noir legends and the second takes him back to *The Maltese Falcon* where his own legend began.

Cook's film-mates from *The Killing*, Marie Windsor, and Timothy Carey joined him in *The Outfit*. Windsor was looking good, a credit to her off-screen Mormon spirituality, while Timmy was still playing with guns.

Legends Jane Greer (*Out of the Past*, 1947) and Robert Ryan (*Act of Violence*, 1948) have larger roles, with Ryan as the villain in a quality neo-noir with the bonus of great nostalgia.

The verdict: *The Outfit.* ★★★⯪☆

Three clue hunters: Cabbie Eli (Cook) writer/ sleuth Dashiell Hammett (Frederic Forrest) and librarian/mystery woman Kit (Marilu Henner).

I enjoyed *Hammett* when I watched it without reading about the brouhaha of its construction. Here are the bare bones without prejudice. Hammett was German director Wim Wenders' first American movie (pre-neo-noir classic *Paris Texas* 1984.) Wenders shot it all on location. Producer Francis Ford Coppola didn't like the result and remember the producer is the Godfather of movie making. With little money left, Wenders shot everything again in the studio. Fewer than a dozen location scenes made it into the movie. In 2015, Wenders went to make a director's cut, and he discovered all the discarded location footage was gone. It is a sad tale, and I would love to see the footage found and a director's cut made. Still, what we have is enjoyable.

In a contemporary review *New York Times* critic Vincent Canby asked,
"Why make a fiction film about the man who virtually invented the low-life private-eye genre with such novels as *The Maltese Falcon* and *The Glass Key*?"
Canby V. *Wim Wenders' Hammett, NYT* July 1, 1983, Section C, page 8.
Had anyone asked me I would have voted, yes. Hammett was a Pinkerton detective agent before he became a writer. The characters he depicted in *The Maltese Falcon* were based on unscrupulous criminals he had met. *Hammett* is shot in murky colors as it tells the tale of Hammett trying to separate facts from the fictions people have created of themselves.

Crystal Springs:
Little-known actor Lydia Lei (*Vice Squad* 1982) was good as femme fatale Crystal Ling.

Peter Boyle (*Taxi Driver* 1976) effectively plays the friend in need who may not be the friend indeed.

Low-budget noir filmmaker Samuel Fuller has a cameo.

The Verdict: *Hammett* ★★★⯨☆

If you enjoyed this book, you might like to place a review at your favorite bookstore.

Enjoyed *Man Of A Thousand Fails*.

Dive deeper into the shadows of classic Hollywood with my other books.

Discover the **Photo-Rich Series**:

• *Noir Dirt Cheap*
• *Film Noir Fate Vs The Working Stiff*
• *Starry Starry Noir Rebels And Censors*
• *Three Faces of Noir Curse Crime Cringe*

Enjoy my **Standalone Film Biographies**:

• *TY, Thel*
• *Man of a Thousand Fails*

Epilogue

An epilogue is an addendum to a book that brings closure.
At right is part of closing credits of 1979's *And Justice for All*.

Disillusioned lawyer Al Pacino sits on the steps outside court. He is confused because he has just seen what might present a shred of optimism in a dystopian world.

The last movie of the man of a thousand fails was an HBO cable television production *The Man Who Broke 1,000 Chains* 1987. Cook – without the Jr. – was well down the cast list, but, on entrance, wordlessly commanded the screen as an old convict. As with *The Maltese Falcon*, almost 50 years earlier, his character had a name that fitted. Then it was Wilmer Cook, now it was Pappy Glue. He had a memorable line. "Half the cons in here didn't do it. But me, I done it."

The Falcon and 1,000 Chains were humble movies, budget-wise, but Cook's interactions with the stars helped the careers of Bogie and Val Kilmer (the neo-noirs *Kill Me Again* 1989, *Thunderheart* 1992, *True Romance* 1993, and *Heat* 1995).

A great strength of film noir was its deployment of character actors, and one of the most loved of those performers was Elisha Cook, who, to his fans, will always be Jr.

The verdict: *The career of Elisha Cook Jr.* 

Selected bibliography

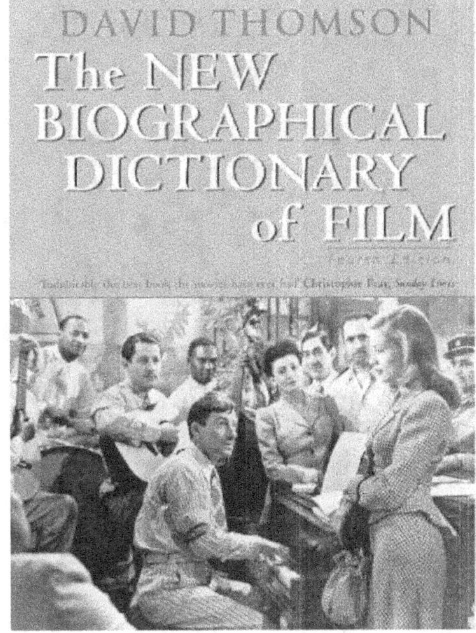

8 Film policier - Film criminel
Un Nouveau genre "policier" :
l'aventure criminelle (cinémas
nationaux ou genre)
Auteur : Nino Frank
L'Écran Français, 28 August 1946

Little
Caesar
Burnett
Little
Caesar
W.R.
Burnett

THE ASPHALT JUNGLE
BY
W. R. BURNETT
HIS BEST NOVEL SINCE "LITTLE CAESAR"

Backstory
INTERVIEWS WITH SCREENWRITERS
OF HOLLYWOOD'S GOLDEN AGE
PAT McGILLIGAN